THE OFFICIAL Disney Parks CELEBRATION COOKBOOK

101 Festival Recipes from the Delicious Disney Vault

PAM BRANDON & THE DISNEY CHEFS

Disney EDITIONS

Los Angeles • New York

Editorial Director: Wendy Lefkon
Senior Editor: Jennifer Eastwood
Designers: Lindsay Broderick and Catalina Castro
Managing Editor: Monica Vasquez
Production: Marybeth Tregarthen

ISBN 978-1-368-09117-6
FAC-025393-24338
Printed in China
First Hardcover Edition, September 2024
1 3 5 7 9 10 8 6 4 2

Visit www.disneybooks.com

THIS PAGE: Spaceship Earth aglow at EPCOT at the Walt Disney World Resort, 2021.

FOLLOWING PAGES: A close-up of the iconic geometric tiles of Spaceship Earth, 2020.

CONTENTS

INTRODUCTION
DELICIOUS DISNEY
FESTIVALS

WHILE DISNEY FESTIVALS are delightfully orchestrated days of live entertainment, art, culture, and beauty, for many guests, the food is the star, the raison d'être. The idea for the very first festival was sparked in the 1980s, when Walt Disney World Resort debuted a four-day wine festival hosted at the Lake Buena Vista Shopping Village, the earliest forerunner of today's EPCOT International Food & Wine Festival. The first festival at EPCOT was the International Flower & Garden Festival, which ran for just 38 days in the spring of 1994 and was lauded for its gorgeous displays of Disney topiaries and curated gardens—but food was not part of the festivities. That same year, the EPCOT International Festival of Holidays (then known as Holidays Around the World) presented the first Candlelight Processional at EPCOT in the America Gardens Theatre, having previously performed in the Magic Kingdom.

It was 1996 when the EPCOT International Food & Wine Festival was introduced, a thirty-day festival with surely one of the world's most spectacular backdrops for a stellar food-and-wine event. During those early years, the roster of celebrity chefs read like a who's who in the culinary world, with intimate winemaker dinners (Julia Child made an appearance), small seminars, and twenty-five Marketplaces around World Showcase Lagoon.

Fast-forward to 2017 with the debut of EPCOT International Festival of the Arts, where edible works of art competed with visual and performing arts, a trifecta of beauty. The festival opens each year in January, the prettiest time of year, when temperatures are cool and conditions are just right for strolling around World Showcase. And the chefs really shine as they create their own masterpieces for this smaller festival.

Traversing to Disneyland Park, the very first Disney California Adventure Food & Wine Festival opened in 2006, a celebration of

California's incredible bounty, with Festival Marketplaces, culinary demonstrations, classes, and winemaker receptions that extend from the park to the Disneyland Resort hotels.

The smaller Lunar New Year at Disney California Adventure Park was first celebrated in January 2013, filled with auspicious wishes for health, luck, and prosperity. Lively entertainment, kid-friendly crafts and activities, and special spots like the Lucky Wishing Wall create a festive, monthlong celebration, where delectable food showcases Chinese, Korean, and Vietnamese cultures.

And the Disney Festival of Holidays, which debuted in 2016, wraps up each year, with diverse celebrations including Christmas, Navidad, Hanukkah, Diwali, Kwanzaa, and Three Kings' Day. Spectacular holiday decor, entertainment (meet Santa Claus!), and the Festive Foods Marketplace make Disney California Adventure Park the perfect place to celebrate the winter holidays.

Ask any guest today, and they'll tell you the number one reason they love the festivals is the cuisine—a chance to share a small plate, or taste an innovative dish, or just to sip and stroll in the parks. Favorites may return, but there's always something new. It's a whole new way to experience Disney.

PREVIOUS PAGES: Minnie Mouse and Mickey Mouse at Disney California Adventure during Disney Festival of Holidays, 2022.

ABOVE: Chef Mickey at the entrance to Goofy's Kitchen at the Disneyland Hotel (top, 2017), along with a former Hidden Mickey pot-and-pans display (middle). Young Disneyland Resort guests participate in a Jr. Chef event at the Disney California Adventure Food & Wine Festival (bottom, 2018).

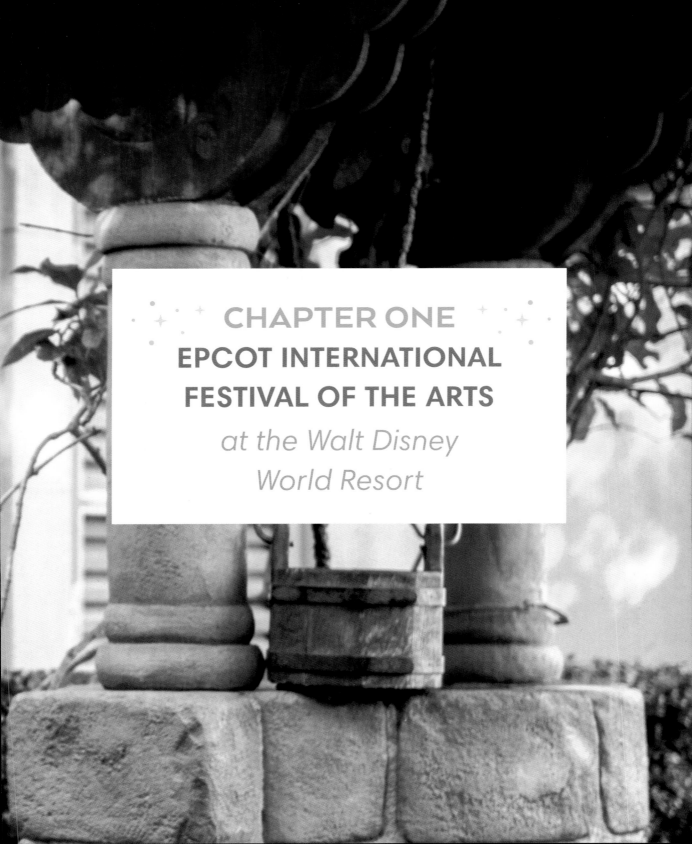

CHAPTER ONE
EPCOT INTERNATIONAL FESTIVAL OF THE ARTS
at the Walt Disney World Resort

WHEN THE EPCOT International Festival of the Arts launched in 2017, the chefs focused on whimsical twists to their creations in Food Studios around World Showcase Lagoon, in the spirit of a festival that celebrates visual, performing, and culinary arts. The food is as big as the Broadway entertainment, and visual arts are celebrated with artists creating works throughout the park.

THESE PAGES: For the 2017 EPCOT International Festival of the Arts, animated Disney sidekicks "created" artwork of their story's hero, resulting in playful displays around World Showcase. Doc painted Snow White's portrait for the Germany pavilion (previous pages); Mushu charred a scene with Mulan for the China pavilion (above); and Flora and Merryweather teamed up (sort of) on a picture of Aurora for the France pavilion (opposite). *For more from this fanciful art series, see page 27.*

CHORIZO EMPANADA WITH SPICY TURMERIC AND ANNATTO AÏOLI

Chorizo makes a hearty filling, with onions and peppers for crunch in this savory turnover. The best part might be the bright yellow turmeric aïoli and annatto mayo for drizzling or dipping. Annatto is a nutty, floral spice often used in Central American cuisine, mildly sweet and spicy with earthy notes.

MAKES 10–12

INTRODUCED 2021 • VIBRANTE & VÍVIDO: ENCANTO COCINA FOOD STUDIO

EMPANADA DOUGH

3 cups all-purpose flour

1½ teaspoons coarse salt

½ cup cold vegetable shortening, cut into cubes

1 egg yolk, beaten

1 cup ice water, divided

FOR EMPANADA DOUGH

1 Combine flour and salt in a large mixing bowl. Add shortening and mix with hands until the flour mixture resembles a coarse meal.

2 Combine egg yolk with ½ cup ice water in a small bowl. Add to flour mixture and stir with wooden spoon until soft dough forms. Slowly add up to an additional ½ cup ice water if dough is too dry.

3 Transfer dough to a floured surface and knead 5 to 6 times. Divide into two pieces, forming each into a disk. Wrap with plastic wrap and refrigerate 30 minutes.

(RECIPE CONTINUES ON PAGE 6)

OPPOSITE, BOTTOM: Spaceship Earth shimmering in the sunlight at EPCOT at the Walt Disney World Resort, 2020.

CHORIZO EMPANADA WITH SPICY TURMERIC AND ANNATTO AÏOLI

(CONTINUED)

FOR CHORIZO FILLING

1. Heat large sauté pan over medium heat for 5 minutes, until hot. Add chorizo and cook fully, breaking into small pieces, for 8 to 10 minutes. Then add onions and poblano peppers; cook for 8 minutes, until soft but not browned.

2. Stir in flour and mix 1 to 2 minutes, until roux forms. Add diced tomatoes and bring to a boil. Reduce heat to low and simmer for 10 minutes. If mixture becomes too thick, add 1 to 2 tablespoons water at a time.

3. Remove from heat. Stir in cilantro and season with salt and pepper, to taste. Cool for 15 minutes.

FOR SPICY TURMERIC AÏOLI

Combine mayonnaise, sriracha, and turmeric in a small bowl. Refrigerate until ready to serve.

FOR ANNATTO AÏOLI

Combine mayonnaise, ground annatto, and red food coloring, if desired, in a small bowl. Refrigerate until ready to serve.

CHORIZO FILLING

¾ pound ground chorizo

1 cup diced Spanish onion

1 cup diced poblano pepper

1 tablespoon all-purpose flour

1 (14½-ounce) can diced tomatoes

Water, as needed

1½ teaspoons finely chopped fresh cilantro

Coarse salt and freshly ground black pepper, to taste

SPICY TURMERIC AÏOLI

½ cup mayonnaise

1½ teaspoons sriracha

½ teaspoon ground turmeric

ANNATTO AÏOLI

½ cup mayonnaise

½ teaspoon ground annatto

Red food coloring, if desired

OPPOSITE: Guests could walk into displays inspired by world-famous masterpieces for personal photos at the 2018 EPCOT International Festival of the Arts.

FOR CHORIZO EMPANADAS

1   Preheat oven to 400°F. Roll out one disk of dough on a large floured surface until it is ⅛ inch thick. Using a 5-inch round cookie cutter, cut into 5 to 6 circles. Repeat with remaining dough.

2   Beat egg and water together in a small bowl. Set aside.

3   Place 3 tablespoons of the Chorizo Filling in the center of each dough circle. Brush egg mixture on the outer edge of the dough. Fold together to make a half-moon shape. Seal with a fork or crimping tool.

4   Place empanadas on ungreased baking sheet. Bake for 25 minutes, until golden brown. Drizzle Spicy Turmeric Aïoli and Annatto Aïoli over each empanada. Garnish with cilantro.

CHORIZO EMPANADAS

Empanada Dough

1 egg, beaten

1 tablespoon water

Chorizo Filling

Spicy Turmeric Aïoli

Annatto Aïoli

¼ cup fresh cilantro leaves, torn or chopped

BLUE CORN PUPUSA STUFFED WITH CHEESE AND TOPPED WITH SHREDDED PORK

MAINS & SIDES

A pupusa is a thick griddle cake. It takes a while to make this Salvadoran specialty, but it's worth the effort.

MAKES 8

INTRODUCED 2021 • VIBRANTE & VÍVIDO: ENCANTO COCINA FOOD STUDIO

FOR PORK WITH GUAJILLO-ÁRBOL CHILE SAUCE

1. Remove stems from guajillo and árbol chiles. Heat large sauté pan over medium heat for 5 minutes, until hot. Add chiles and toast for 1 to 2 minutes on each side, until darker in color.

2. Place chiles in large pot with 6 cups water and garlic clove. Bring to simmer and cook, covered, for 20 minutes, until soft. Blend with immersion blender until smooth.

3. Season pork generously with salt. Add to pot of water. Bring to boil. Reduce to a simmer and cook, covered, for 1 hour, until pork is tender. Remove from liquid and cool for 20 minutes. Do not discard cooking liquid.

4. Combine 2 tablespoons water with cornstarch in a small bowl. Bring pork liquid back to a boil. Add cornstarch and water mixture and stir until sauce thickens. Reduce heat to low.

5. Shred pork and add to sauce. Season with additional salt, to taste. Keep warm until ready to serve.

PORK WITH GUAJILLO-ÁRBOL CHILE SAUCE

6 dried guajillo chiles

1 árbol chile

6 cups, plus 2 tablespoons, water, divided

1 garlic clove

2–3 pounds pork butt, cut into 1½-inch pieces

Coarse salt, to taste

2 tablespoons cornstarch

(RECIPE CONTINUES ON PAGE 10)

BLUE CORN PUPUSA STUFFED WITH CHEESE AND TOPPED WITH SHREDDED PORK

(CONTINUED)

FOR CABBAGE SLAW

1. Combine apple cider vinegar, water, salt, oregano, brown sugar, and red pepper flakes in a small saucepan. Bring to boil over medium heat and cook, stirring frequently, until sugar dissolves. Remove from heat and cool to room temperature.

2. Mix shredded cabbage, onions, and carrots in large bowl. Add cooled dressing and toss to coat.

3. Refrigerate for at least 4 hours, or for up to one day, before serving. Season with salt and pepper, to taste.

FOR AJI AMARILLO CREAM

Combine sour cream, aji amarillo paste, lime juice, and salt in a medium-sized bowl. Season with additional salt, to taste. Refrigerate until ready to serve.

CABBAGE SLAW

½ cup apple cider vinegar

¼ cup water

½ teaspoon coarse salt, plus more to taste

¼ teaspoon dried oregano

¾ teaspoon brown sugar

Pinch red pepper flakes

2 cups shredded red cabbage

½ red onion, thinly sliced

1 carrot, julienned

Freshly ground black pepper, to taste

AJI AMARILLO CREAM

1 cup sour cream

2¾ teaspoons aji amarillo paste

1 tablespoon fresh lime juice

1 teaspoon coarse salt, plus more to taste

LEFT: For the 2019 EPCOT International Festival of the Arts, guests could join Disney artists in painting on canvases set up around World Showcase.

FOR BLUE CORN PUPUSA

1. Line a baking sheet with parchment paper. Spray with nonstick cooking spray and set aside.

2. Combine masa, garlic powder, onion powder, and salt in mixing bowl. Pour in ¾ cups water and stir to combine. Slowly add up to an additional ¾ cup water, ¼ cup at a time, until a soft, pliable dough forms.

3. Scoop dough into ¼-cup balls and place on reserved baking sheet.

4. Using your fingers, make a well in the center of each ball of dough. Fill each well with 1 tablespoon Cheddar cheese. Pinch to close dough around the well.

5. Gently flatten into disks, making sure no cheese is showing.

6. With caution, heat canola oil in large nonstick skillet over medium heat for 5 minutes. Cook pupusa for 2 to 3 minutes on each side, until dark blue in color and crispy on the outside. Keep warm until ready to serve.

TO SERVE

Place pupusa in the center of each plate. Top with pork and red cabbage slaw. Then drizzle aji amarillo cream on top, and garnish with cilantro.

BLUE CORN PUPUSA

2 cups blue corn masa

⅛ teaspoon garlic powder

¼ teaspoon onion powder

1 teaspoon coarse salt

1½ cups water, divided

½ cup grated white Cheddar cheese

¼ cup canola oil

GARNISH

16 fresh cilantro leaves

RIGHT: For the 2022 EPCOT International Festival of the Arts, Disney Fine Art kiosks featured pieces created especially for the show, including this Figment print by Trevor Carlton.

SPICY AJIACO (COLOMBIAN CHICKEN AND POTATO STEW)

STARTERS & SMALL PLATES

Bold South American flavors with a real kick from the guajillo and árbol chiles. The fresh corn, creamy avocado, and crème fraîche add a cooling finish.

SERVES 4

INTRODUCED 2023 • VIBRANTE & VÍVIDO: ENCANTO COCINA FOOD STUDIO

FOR CHICKEN-POTATO MIXTURE

1. To make a marinade, remove stems from chiles. Toast in a dry hot pan until slightly darker in color.

2. Place in a pot with water, garlic cloves, and salt. Bring to a simmer over medium heat and cook at least 20 minutes or until soft and pliable.

3. Remove from heat and blend with an immersion blender. Chill until ready to use.

4. When sauce is cooled, add 1 cup to a zip-top bag with chicken, and marinate for several hours or overnight. (Keep remaining sauce for serving.)

5. Preheat oven to 350°F. Place chicken on a greased baking sheet and bake until internal temperature reaches 165°F. Cool and shred chicken.

6. Mix shredded chicken with diced potatoes and remaining chili sauce.

FOR SPICY AJIACO

Add ½ cup Chicken-Potato Mixture to each of four serving bowls. Add ¼ ear corn to each, and top with 1 cup hot chicken broth. Add ¼ cup diced avocado. Top each with 1 tablespoon crème fraîche, 1 teaspoon capers, and chili threads, if using, for garnish. Serve hot.

CHICKEN-POTATO MIXTURE

3 dried guajillo chiles

1 small dried árbol chile

2 cups water

2 garlic cloves

2 teaspoons coarse salt

1 pound boneless, skinless chicken thighs

2 medium white potatoes, peeled, cooked, and diced

SPICY AJIACO

2 cups Chicken-Potato Mixture, divided

2 ears corn, cooked and quartered, divided

4 cups hot chicken stock, divided

1 cup diced avocado, divided

¼ cup crème fraîche, divided

4 teaspoons capers, divided

Chili threads, for optional garnish

OPPOSITE, BOTTOM: Disney artists drew detailed sidewalk chalk drawings throughout the park, including Figment near the IMAGINATION! pavilion, at the 2019 EPCOT International Festival of the Arts.

DUCK AND DUMPLINGS

STARTERS & SMALL PLATES

So many layers of flavor and texture in this elegant dish featuring duck and soft ricotta dumplings. EPCOT chefs finish the duck in a smoker, but it's just as delicious pan-fried.

SERVES 2

INTRODUCED 2023 • THE ARTIST'S TABLE FOOD STUDIO

FOR DUCK HAM

1 Combine the first nine ingredients in a large pot. Bring to a simmer over medium-high heat, stirring to dissolve salt and sugar.

2 Remove from heat and cool to room temperature. Refrigerate until completely chilled.

3 Add duck breast to the chilled brine and weight down with a plate. Refrigerate and brine 12 to 16 hours.

4 Rinse breasts under cold water and pat dry. Refrigerate on a rack set over a small baking sheet to dry for several hours or overnight.

5 Remove from refrigerator at least 20 minutes before cooking. Using a sharp kitchen knife, cut 5 to 6 even slashes across the skin of the duck breast (be careful not to cut into meat). Season with salt and pepper.

6 Heat a heavy skillet over medium-high heat. Lay duck breast skin side down; it should sizzle when it hits the pan. Cook for 4 minutes. Turn and cook 4 minutes. Flip back to skin side down and cook for 2 minutes, then flip and cook another 4 minutes or until internal temperature reaches 140°F. Remove from pan and cover with aluminum foil to rest.

DUCK HAM

8 cups water

½ cup coarse salt

½ cup sugar

2 teaspoons pink salt

½ cup maple syrup

½ cup sherry

½ teaspoon thyme

1 bay leaf

½ teaspoon juniper berry

2 pounds skin-on duck breast

Coarse salt and freshly ground black pepper, to taste

CELERY ROOT PURÉE

1 pound celery root (1–2 roots), diced

½ cup milk

½ cup heavy cream

Coarse salt and white pepper, to taste

FOR CELERY ROOT PURÉE

1 Cover celery root with milk in a saucepan over medium heat. Bring to a simmer and cook until celery root is tender, about 1 hour.

2 Remove from heat and purée in blender until smooth with about ¼ cup heavy cream, adding more as needed to make purée silky smooth. Season with salt and pepper.

FOR RICOTTA DUMPLINGS

1 Combine ricotta, Parmesan, egg yolk, and salt in a large bowl. Gently mix in flour (don't overmix; it will make dumplings tough).

2 Dust a parchment-lined rimmed baking sheet with flour. Scoop out a tablespoonful of dough and roll into a loose ball with floured hands. Repeat with all the dough.

3 Bring a large pot of salted water to a steady boil. Gently lower dumplings into water and cook until they rise to the surface, about 5 minutes. Don't crowd the pot; cook in batches if necessary. Texture will go from dense to light and pillowy.

4 Remove from water with a slotted spoon and mix with a little of the duck demi-glace.

DUCK AND DUMPLINGS

To serve, lightly sauté carrots and turnips in butter, if using. Season with salt and pepper. On serving plate add a generous spoonful of Celery Root Purée, then top with 3 dumplings and slices of Duck Ham. Garnish with carrots and turnips, if using. Serve hot.

RICOTTA DUMPLINGS

1 cup ricotta cheese

½ cup Parmesan cheese

1 large egg yolk

1 teaspoon salt

2 tablespoons flour

Favorite duck demi-glace

DUCK AND DUMPLINGS

Petite carrots and turnips, optional

Unsalted butter, to taste

Coarse salt and freshly ground black pepper, to taste

1 cup Celery Root Purée

6 Ricotta Dumplings

3–4 slices Duck Ham

BLOOD ORANGE-BRAISED BEET TARTARE WITH MUSTARD VINAIGRETTE, PICKLED MUSHROOMS, AND GOLDEN BEETS

STARTERS & SMALL PLATES

Inspired by beef tartare, this refreshing vegetarian version stars roasted red and yellow beets with wild mushrooms and a flourish of pumpkin seeds.

SERVES 4

INTRODUCED 2023 • GOURMET LANDSCAPES FOOD STUDIO

FOR FRENCH MUSTARD VINAIGRETTE

Whisk together mustard and vinegar. Slowly whisk in olive oil. Add tarragon and salt. Set aside until ready to use.

FOR BLOOD ORANGE-BRAISED BEETS

1. Preheat oven to 300°F. Rinse beets, trim off leafy tops, and peel. Place in roasting pan and add remaining ingredients, except the vinaigrette. Cover tightly with foil and roast for 2 hours or until tender and easily pierced with the tip of a paring knife.

2. Remove from oven and cool. Then dice into small pieces and set aside. Mix with French Mustard Vinaigrette and refrigerate until ready to use.

FOR BRAISED GOLDEN BEETS

Preheat oven to 300°F. Rinse beets, trim off leafy tops, and peel. Place in roasting pan and add remaining ingredients. Cover tightly with foil and roast for 2 hours or until tender and easily pierced with the tip of a paring knife. Then remove from oven and cool. Dice small for serving.

FRENCH MUSTARD VINAIGRETTE

2 teaspoons stone-ground mustard

¼ cup sherry vinegar

¼ cup olive oil

½ teaspoon chopped fresh tarragon

¼ teaspoon coarse salt

BLOOD ORANGE-BRAISED BEETS

2 large whole red beets

2 cups water

½ cup blood orange purée

1 tablespoon Herbes de Provence

2 teaspoons finely minced fresh garlic

1 teaspoon finely minced shallot

1 teaspoon coarse salt

½ teaspoon freshly ground black pepper

French Mustard Vinaigrette, to taste

FOR WILD MUSHROOMS WITH VINAIGRETTE

Heat canola oil in a small saucepan over medium heat. Add shallots and sauté for 2 to 3 minutes. Add mushrooms, vinegar, and truffle oil and sauté for 2 to 3 minutes. Then turn off heat. Add salt, pepper, and thyme, and cool.

FOR SPICED PUMPKIN SEEDS

Preheat oven to 300°F. Spread seeds on rimmed baking sheet and roast until fragrant, about 10 minutes. Remove from oven and toss with paprika, cayenne, and salt. Cool to room temperature.

TO SERVE

Place Blood Orange–Braised Beets into 4 single-serving, rectangular molds to create "tartare." Place on 4 serving plates. Evenly divide remaining ingredients and top with Braised Golden Beets, a drizzle of Wild Mushrooms with Vinaigrette, Spiced Pumpkin Seeds, vegan blue cheese crumbles, and sorrel leaves.

BRAISED GOLDEN BEETS

1 golden beet

½ cup champagne vinegar

½ cup water

2 tablespoons thinly sliced shallot

½ teaspoon crushed fresh garlic

Sprig fresh thyme

WILD MUSHROOMS WITH VINAIGRETTE

1 tablespoon canola oil

1 teaspoon minced shallots

½ cup mixed wild mushrooms, cleaned and chopped

½ cup champagne vinegar

½ teaspoon truffle oil

1 teaspoon coarse salt

⅓ teaspoon freshly ground black pepper

⅓ teaspoon dry thyme

SPICED PUMPKIN SEEDS

½ cup unsalted roasted pumpkin seeds

½ teaspoon smoked paprika

½ teaspoon cayenne pepper

¼ teaspoon coarse salt

ADDITIONAL TOPPINGS

Vegan blue cheese crumbles, to taste

Sorrel leaves, to taste

CHOCOFLAN

This recipe begins and ends with decadent cajeta, or dulce de leche, to create a creamy Mexican custard and chocolate sponge cake. The topping is a simple spread of dulce de leche and crunchy hazelnuts.

SERVES 12

INTRODUCED 2019 • EL ARTISTA HAMBRIENTO FOOD STUDIO

CHOCOFLAN

¼ cup cajeta

1½ cups all-purpose flour

6 tablespoons unsweetened cocoa powder

1 teaspoon baking soda

1 teaspoon baking powder

10½ tablespoons unsalted butter, softened

1 cup sugar

5 eggs, divided

2 tablespoons brewed espresso, cooled

1 cup whole milk

1 (12-ounce) can evaporated milk

1 (14-ounce) can sweetened condensed milk

1 teaspoon vanilla extract

FOR CHOCOFLAN

1 Preheat oven to 350°F. Spray a 9 × 13-inch baking pan with nonstick cooking spray. Set aside.

2 Place cajeta in microwave-safe bowl and cook, stirring every 15 seconds, for 45 seconds to 1 minute, until cajeta pours easily. Spread and evenly coat bottom of a prepared baking pan.

3 Mix flour, cocoa powder, baking soda, and baking powder in a medium-sized mixing bowl. Set aside.

4 Cream butter in the bowl of an electric mixer fitted with a paddle attachment until smooth. Add sugar, and cream until fluffy. Beat in 1 egg and cooled espresso until smooth.

5 Add half of the flour mixture and ½ cup milk and mix on low speed. Repeat with remaining flour and milk; blend until smooth.

6 Spread over top of cajeta in prepared pan and set aside.

7 Combine evaporated milk, sweetened condensed milk, vanilla extract, and remaining 4 eggs in blender and purée until smooth and fluffy. Evenly pour over cake batter.

8 Place 9 × 13-inch pan in larger baking pan and fill larger pan with water until ⅓ full.

9 Bake 50 to 55 minutes or until knife inserted in center of cake comes out clean. Remove from water bath and cool for 1 hour.

TO SERVE

1 When cool, run knife around the edge of cake. Place large baking sheet on top of pan and flip pan to release cake. Cut the cake in half, making 2 rectangles, approximately 9 × 6 inches each. Place 1 rectangle, cake side down, on a platter using two spatulas. Top with second rectangle.

2 Warm 1 cup cajeta in microwave for 1 minute, until warm. Spread on top of Chocoflan and sprinkle with hazelnuts. Then cut into squares, and dust top with powdered sugar before serving.

TOPPING

1 cup cajeta

¼ cup hazelnuts, crushed

¼ cup powdered sugar

PASSION FRUIT MOUSSE WITH DRAGON FRUIT JAM

Almost too pretty to eat, this Latin American–inspired sweet takes a little time, but the tart passion fruit and sweet dragon fruit are a happy combination. (You can always skip baking the sugar cookies and use your favorite store-bought brand.)

SERVES 12

INTRODUCED 2021 • VIBRANTE & VÍVIDO: ENCANTO COCINA FOOD STUDIO

DRAGON FRUIT JAM

1 (12-ounce) bag frozen red dragon fruit

1 cup sugar

1 tablespoon lime juice

PASSION FRUIT MOUSSE

¼ cup sugar

1 cup passion fruit purée

1 cup chopped white chocolate

1½ cups heavy whipping cream

Dragon Fruit Jam

FOR DRAGON FRUIT JAM

1. Combine dragon fruit, sugar, and lime juice in a small saucepan. Cook over medium-high heat until liquid begins to boil. Reduce to simmer and cook for 20 minutes, stirring occasionally, until thick.

2. Place in a medium-sized bowl and cool for 30 minutes. Blend with an immersion blender until smooth. Refrigerate until ready to use.

FOR PASSION FRUIT MOUSSE

1. Combine sugar and passion fruit purée in a small saucepan. Cook over medium heat for 5 minutes, until hot but not boiling.

2. Place white chocolate in a medium-sized glass bowl. Pour hot passion fruit mixture on top and let rest for 2 minutes. Stir until chocolate is melted and mixture is smooth.

3. Cover and refrigerate for at least 4 hours.

4 Whip heavy cream in the bowl of an electric mixer fitted with a whisk attachment until stiff peaks form. Gently fold whipped cream into chilled passion fruit mixture.

5 Transfer mousse to a piping bag fitted with a large round tip. Then fill twelve 3¼ × 2⅛ × 1¼-inch rectangular silicone molds halfway full with mousse.

6 Pour reserved Dragon Fruit Jam into a piping bag fitted with a small round tip. Carefully pipe a thick strip of jam into the center of each mold, being careful to avoid the edges.

7 Fill each mold with remaining mousse, filling to the top. Freeze for a least 4 hours, or overnight.

(RECIPE CONTINUES ON PAGE 22)

PASSION FRUIT MOUSSE WITH DRAGON FRUIT JAM

(CONTINUED)

FOR SUGAR COOKIES

1. Cream together butter and sugar in the bowl of an electric mixer fitted with a paddle attachment. Add eggs and vanilla extract and beat on medium speed until mixed. Add flour, baking powder, and salt, and mix on low speed until soft dough forms.

2. Cover and chill dough in refrigerator for at least one hour.

3. Preheat oven to 325°F. Line 2 baking sheets with silicone baking mats.

4. Roll dough on a floured surface into a ¼-inch-thick rectangle. Cut into twelve 3½ × 2½-inch rectangles.

5. Place 6 cookies on each baking sheet. Bake 12 to 15 minutes, until golden brown. Cool completely.

6. Once cookies are cool, place all 12 cookies on a parchment-lined baking sheet. Set aside.

FOR DRAGON FRUIT GLAZE

1. Bloom gelatin sheets in ice water. When ready, heat dragon fruit and sugar in a small saucepan over medium heat until boiling.

2. Drain excess water from gelatin sheets. Then add gelatin and sweetened condensed milk to boiling sugar mixture.

3. Place chopped white chocolate in a large bowl. Pour warm mixture over white chocolate. Let sit for 2 minutes.

4. Carefully blend with an immersion blender until chocolate and dragon fruit are smooth. Cool to 90°F.

SUGAR COOKIES

¾ cups unsalted butter, softened

1 cup sugar

2 eggs

½ teaspoon vanilla extract

2½ cups all-purpose flour

1 teaspoon baking powder

½ teaspoon salt

DRAGON FRUIT GLAZE

15 gelatin sheets

2 cups ice water

1¼ cups frozen red dragon fruit

1½ cups sugar

1 (14-ounce) can sweetened condensed milk

4 cups chopped white chocolate

FOR PASSION FRUIT SYRUP

Place passion fruit purée, lime juice, and sugar in a small saucepan. Cook over medium-low heat, until boiling. Simmer for 5 minutes, until sauce thickens and begins to reduce. Then remove from heat, and cool to room temperature before use.

TO SERVE

1   Remove frozen mousse from molds. Place on baking sheet lined with silicone baking mat.

2   Pour 2½ cups of the 90°F Dragon Fruit Glaze into a liquid measuring cup. Carefully pour on top of the frozen mousse, making sure edges and sides are covered. Set in refrigerator for 30 minutes.

3   Reheat remaining glaze in a saucepan over low heat until it reaches 90°F. Pour into liquid measuring cup and pour over mousse for a second coat.

4   Place one mousse onto the center of each cookie. If mousse is too soft, place in freezer for 10 minutes before moving. Refrigerate until ready to serve.

5   Place 1 tablespoon Passion Fruit Syrup on each plate. Spread evenly into a circle with a pastry brush or by pressing the flat edge of a drinking glass against the syrup.

6   Place cookie on the back edge of the sauce. If desired, serve with mini face masks made from gum paste.

PASSION FRUIT SYRUP

⅔ cup passion fruit purée

1 tablespoon lime juice

½ cup sugar

DECORATION

Gum paste, shaped into mini face masks, and colored with food coloring as desired

RIGHT: For the 2022 EPCOT International Festival of the Arts, a whimsical highlight included a commemorative Figment Spork.

HUMMINGBIRD CAKE

Here's a recipe where you can make just the cake (it's delicious unfrosted) or just the cake and icing— or get fancy with toasted coconut, caramelized pineapple, and banana sorbet. The tangy banana sorbet is a nice complement to the extra-sweet cake with a rich cream cheese frosting (said to be named after the bird because it's sweet enough to attract hummingbirds). The toasted coconut on top adds a nice finish.

MAKES 1 (8 × 8) CAKE

INTRODUCED 2023 • THE ARTIST'S TABLE FOOD STUDIO

CAKE

2½ cups flour

1 cup sugar

¼ teaspoon salt

¾ teaspoon baking soda

¼ teaspoon ground cinnamon

1 egg

¾ cup canola oil

1½ teaspoons vanilla extract

½ canned pineapple tidbits

2 bananas, mashed

½ cup chopped pecans, optional

FOR CAKE

1   Preheat oven to 325°F. Grease an 8 × 8 baking pan. Combine flour, sugar, salt, baking soda, and cinnamon in a large bowl. Set aside.

2   Stir together egg, canola oil, and vanilla in the bowl of a stand mixer (or use a hand mixer). Add dry ingredients and mix on medium speed until fully combined; add pineapple and bananas and mix on medium speed until combined. Stir in pecans.

3   Transfer batter to prepared pan, smoothing top. Bake for 55 minutes, or until a toothpick inserted in the center comes out clean. Remove from oven and cool completely before icing.

OPPOSITE, BOTTOM: Guests contribute to large paint-by-number wall murals, including these lively Figment panels, at the 2019 EPCOT International Festival of the Arts.

(RECIPE CONTINUES ON PAGE 26)

HUMMINGBIRD CAKE

(CONTINUED)

FOR CREAM CHEESE ICING

Combine butter and cream cheese in the bowl of a stand mixer. Beat until lump free. Add vanilla extract and salt and combine. Then with mixer on low speed, gradually add powdered sugar until smooth. Spread evenly over top and sides of cooled cake.

FOR TOASTED COCONUT

Preheat oven to 300°F. Spread coconut on baking sheet. Bake 5 to 10 minutes or until lightly golden brown. Cool completely, then store in a dry container at room temperature until ready to use.

FOR CARAMELIZED COMPOTE

Melt butter in a small saucepan over medium heat. Add pineapple and sprinkle with brown sugar. Baste pineapple with butter–brown sugar mixture, cooking at a low boil for 3 to 4 minutes, or until mixture thickens. Remove from heat and keep at room temperature until ready to use.

FOR BANANA SORBET

Place frozen bananas in food processor with blade attachment. Pulse to create small lumps, using a spatula to spread the mixture out. Continue processing until consistency of smooth, soft-serve ice cream. Can be made in advance and frozen in a zip-top bag.

TO SERVE

Top slice of cake with Toasted Coconut, and add Caramelized Compote either on top or to the side with a scoop of Banana Sorbet.

CREAM CHEESE ICING

½ cup unsalted butter, softened

8 ounces cream cheese, softened

1 teaspoon vanilla extract

½ teaspoon salt

4 cups powdered sugar

TOASTED COCONUT

½ cup shredded coconut

CARAMELIZED COMPOTE

1½ cups unsalted butter

½ cup fresh pineapple or canned pineapple tidbits

½ cup brown sugar

BANANA SORBET

5 very ripe bananas, frozen

OPPOSITE: For the 2017 EPCOT International Festival of the Arts, Maurice from *Beauty and the Beast* (1991) created a contraption to draw a picture of his daughter, Belle, for the France pavilion. *For more from this fanciful art series, see pages xii–1, 2, and 3.*

CHAPTER TWO

DISNEY CALIFORNIA ADVENTURE FOOD & WINE FESTIVAL

at the Disneyland Resort

LAUNCHED IN 2006 to celebrate the incredible bounty of the Golden State, Disney California Adventure Food & Wine Festival focuses on the beautiful produce, artisan cheeses, and vineyards of California. Feast at the Festival Marketplaces, or take time for a special dinner, celebrity chef appearance, or a wine seminar. Plus, there're plenty of family-friendly experiences.

THESE PAGES: The annual Food & Wine Festival of the Disneyland Resort is located all around Disney California Adventure, including meet-and-greet opportunities with favorite characters (previous pages, 2022; opposite, 2018), and a WELCOME sign displayed in front of Grizzly Peak (above, 2022).

GRILLED BEEF TENDERLOIN SLIDERS WITH GARLIC CHIMICHURRI AND PICKLED ONIONS

Garlic is a major California crop, and the garlicky chimichurri for these sliders adds a kick to the buttery tenderloin, with crunchy pickled onions for texture. Pairs well with a Napa Valley cabernet sauvignon.

MAKES 10

INTRODUCED 2017 • GARLIC KISSED FESTIVAL MARKETPLACE

FOR PICKLED ONIONS

1. Mix together all ingredients except onions until sugar dissolves.

2. Place onions in a jar; pour mixture over and refrigerate 24 hours.

FOR GARLIC CHIMICHURRI

1. Preheat oven to 350°F. Drizzle cloves with 1 teaspoon oil, season with salt and pepper, and wrap in aluminum foil. Roast 30 minutes, or until golden brown and soft. Cool 10 minutes, then peel each clove.

2. Heat orange juice in a small saucepan over medium heat until reduced by half. Cool 10 minutes.

3. Place peeled roasted garlic cloves in a small bowl and press with back of spoon until smooth. Discard any hard pieces.

4. Stir together roasted garlic, orange juice, lime juice, remaining ¼ cup canola oil, parsley, red onions, and cayenne pepper in a medium-sized bowl. Season with salt and pepper. Refrigerate until ready to use.

PICKLED ONIONS

¼ cup red wine vinegar

1½ teaspoons sugar

1 teaspoon coarse salt

Pinch dried oregano

½ medium red onion, julienned

GARLIC CHIMICHURRI

1 whole bulb garlic, broken into cloves, unpeeled

¼ cup plus 1 teaspoon canola oil, divided

Coarse salt and freshly ground black pepper, to taste

½ cup orange juice

3 ounces fresh lime juice

½ cup finely chopped flat leaf parsley

½ cup diced red onion

¼ teaspoon ground cayenne pepper

FOR BEEF TENDERLOIN SLIDERS

Season beef tenderloin with salt and pepper. Grill until center reaches medium-rare. Let rest 5 minutes before slicing. Cut slider rolls in half and toast. Set aside.

TO SERVE

Slice tenderloin into 10 equal pieces, about 1 inch thick each. Place one slice of tenderloin on bottom of each slider roll. Top beef with chimichurri and pickled red onions.

BEEF TENDERLOIN SLIDERS

18–20 ounces beef tenderloin

Coarse salt and freshly ground black pepper, to taste

10 slider rolls

KOREAN FRIED CHICKEN SLIDERS

STARTERS & SMALL PLATES

The gochujang sauce and sweet Hawaiian roll are essentials for this trendy sandwich. Make sure the oil is hot enough (around 350°F) when you start frying so the chicken gets crispy.

SERVES 4

INTRODUCED 2023 • STUDIO CATERING CO. FESTIVAL MARKETPLACE

FOR PICKLED RED ONIONS

Cut onion in half and thinly slice. Place in a medium-sized bowl and add seasoned rice vinegar. Cover and refrigerate overnight.

FOR KOREAN FRIED CHICKEN

1 Clean and trim fat from chicken thighs. Cut into 2-ounce portions. Place chicken thighs in a zip-top bag and cover with buttermilk. Refrigerate 2 to 8 hours.

2 Remove from refrigerator and pat dry.

3 With caution, heat canola oil in a deep fryer or Dutch oven to 300°F.

4 Combine potato starch and cornstarch in a small bowl.

5 Coat chicken thighs in starch mixture. Carefully fry chicken for 7 minutes. Drain on wire rack set over a baking sheet.

6 Increase oil temperature to 350°F. Carefully fry chicken a second time for 3 minutes, until chicken is crispy and reaches an internal temperature of 165°F.

7 Drain on wire rack. Keep warm until ready to serve.

PICKLED RED ONIONS

1 medium red onion

1 cup seasoned rice vinegar

KOREAN FRIED CHICKEN

1 pound boneless, skinless chicken thighs, butterflied

1 cup buttermilk

Canola oil, for frying

½ cup potato starch

½ cup cornstarch

KIMCHEE SLAW

½ cup mayonnaise

1 tablespoon sesame oil

½ teaspoon black pepper

2 tablespoons soy sauce

¼ cup sugar

2 tablespoons seasoned rice vinegar

1½ cups shredded green cabbage

¼ cup kimchee

FOR KIMCHEE SLAW

1 Combine mayonnaise, sesame oil, black pepper, soy sauce, sugar, and seasoned rice vinegar in a medium-sized bowl and whisk until smooth.

2 Add cabbage and kimchee and stir to coat. Cover and refrigerate at least 2 hours.

FOR GOCHUJANG SAUCE

Combine all ingredients in a small saucepan. Bring to a simmer over medium heat, then reduce heat and simmer for 5 to 7 minutes, until glaze is shiny. Keep warm until ready to serve.

TO SERVE

Coat chicken with Gochujang Sauce. Place on slider buns and top with Kimchee Slaw and Pickled Red Onions.

GOCHUJANG SAUCE

2 teaspoons minced garlic

¾ teaspoon sriracha

1½ teaspoons honey

½ teaspoon sesame oil

2 teaspoons sugar

½ teaspoon seasoned rice vinegar

½ cup gochujang paste

½ cup water

FOR SERVING

Korean Fried Chicken

Gochujang Sauce

8 Hawaiian-style slider buns

Kimchee Slaw

Pickled Red Onions

CHÈVRE FROMAGE BLANC TARTINE INFUSED WITH ROSEMARY AND HONEY

Sweet and savory in one bite with the punch of rosemary and sweetness of honey: use a good whole-grain bread, thinly sliced, as the base. If you can't find quince paste, fig jam is a good stand-in.

MAKES 10-12 SLICES

INTRODUCED 2017 • NUTS ABOUT CHEESE FESTIVAL MARKETPLACE

CHÈVRE FROMAGE BLANC BLEND

1 cup chèvre fromage blanc

⅓ cup crème fraîche

¼ cup honey

1 teaspoon finely chopped fresh rosemary

CANDIED HAZELNUTS

¾ cup sugar

3 tablespoons water

1 cup hazelnuts, toasted and coarsely chopped

HONEY BUTTER

½ cup unsalted butter, room temperature

¼ cup honey

FOR CHÈVRE FROMAGE BLANC BLEND

Mix together chèvre fromage blanc and crème fraîche in a small bowl until smooth. Add honey and rosemary, stirring well. Cover and refrigerate at least 1 hour.

FOR CANDIED HAZELNUTS

1. Heat sugar and water in a small saucepan over high heat until sugar dissolves. Reduce heat to simmer and cook until amber in color, 5 to 7 minutes.

2. Slowly add hazelnuts, stirring to coat thoroughly. Cook for about 1 minute.

3. Pour nut mixture over nonstick baking mat or parchment-lined baking sheet. Quickly separate nuts to avoid clumping. Set aside to cool.

FOR HONEY BUTTER

Whisk together butter and honey in a small bowl. Cover and set aside. Do not refrigerate.

FOR TARTINE

1 Preheat oven to 350°F. Slice 10 to 12 (½-inch) pieces of bread. Place slices on wire rack on top of rimmed baking sheet.

2 Spread 1 heaping teaspoon Honey Butter on each slice and bake 8 to 10 minutes, until browned and crunchy. Remove from oven and cool completely. Spread about 1 tablespoon quince paste in middle of each slice.

3 Remove cheese mixture from refrigerator. Fill pastry or a zip-top bag (with a snipped corner for piping) with cheese and pipe a thin wavy line of fromage blanc over bread slice and quince paste.

4 Sprinkle each slice with candied chopped hazelnuts and micro basil, if desired.

TARTINE

Whole-grain bread loaf

Honey Butter

6–8 ounces quince paste

Chévre Fromage Blanc Blend

Candied Hazelnuts

Micro basil, optional

WHITE CHEDDAR LAGER SOUP

This soup with white Cheddar and lager is a comfort food classic—use a bread bowl to make it extra fancy, and serve with a tall cold glass of the same amber lager in the recipe.

SERVES 8-10

INTRODUCED 2017 • NUTS ABOUT CHEESE FESTIVAL MARKETPLACE

1 cup salted butter

¾ cup Spanish onion, minced

¾ cup celery, minced

Coarse salt, to taste

½ cup all-purpose flour

4 cups heavy whipping cream

4 cups chicken stock

1½ cups (12 ounces) amber lager

3 cups grated sharp white Cheddar cheese

½ teaspoon ground cayenne pepper

1 teaspoon Worcestershire sauce

Chopped chives, for serving

1. Melt butter in heavy-bottomed pot over medium heat. Add onions and celery. Season with pinch of salt and cook until translucent, 8 to 10 minutes.

2. Add flour and stir to form paste. Cook 3 to 4 minutes, stirring constantly with wire whisk.

3. Slowly add cream and chicken stock, whisking constantly to eliminate lumps. Simmer over low heat for about 30 minutes. (Soup will thicken as it heats.)

4. Whisk in beer and simmer 10 minutes. Remove from heat and cool 10 minutes. Add cheese in batches, stirring constantly until completed melted. Then add cayenne pepper, Worcestershire sauce, and salt, to taste. Top with chives, and serve hot.

GOLDEN BEET SALAD

Golden beets are slightly sweeter than their red counterparts, but either works in this simple salad. Verjus blanc is the tart, fresh juice of unripe grapes—substitute white balsamic vinegar if you can't find verjus blanc. Pair it with a pinot noir from California.

SERVES 5

INTRODUCED 2017 • WINE COUNTRY FESTIVAL MARKETPLACE

FOR VINAIGRETTE

1. Heat verjus blanc to a simmer in a small saucepan over medium heat. Continue simmering for 9 minutes, or until reduced by half. Remove from heat and cool to room temperature.

2. Place mustard in a medium-sized bowl. Slowly pour in cooled verjus blanc, whisking constantly. Slowly whisk in canola oil. Whisk in salt. Refrigerate until ready to use.

FOR GOLDEN BEET SALAD

1. Preheat oven to 350°F. Place beets, canola oil, salt, and pepper in a large bowl, stirring until beets are coated.

2. Tightly wrap beets in aluminum foil.

3. Roast for 15 to 20 minutes, until tender when pierced with a small knife. Remove from oven, open foil, and cool for 30 minutes, or until beets are room temperature.

4. Using a paper towel, remove skin from beets, then trim and slice.

5. Lightly toss beets, arugula, goat cheese, cashews, and raisins in a medium-sized bowl with Vinaigrette, to taste. Season with salt and pepper.

VINAIGRETTE

1 cup verjus blanc

2 teaspoons Dijon mustard

½ cup canola oil

1 teaspoon coarse salt, plus more to taste

GOLDEN BEET SALAD

1 pound baby golden beets

1 tablespoon canola oil

1 teaspoon coarse salt, plus more to taste

¼ teaspoon freshly ground black pepper, plus more to taste

2 cups loosely packed wild baby arugula

½ cup lavender-fennel goat cheese, cubed

¼ cup roasted, salted cashew halves

¼ cup golden raisins

JACKFRUIT CARNITA BANH MI NACHOS WITH CILANTRO CREMA AND "PICKLED" DE GALLO

Jackfruit is often used in vegan dishes to replace barbecued meat, with a texture similar to chicken or pork. Canned or frozen works—just be sure to rinse canned jackfruit before marinating.

SERVES 6

INTRODUCED 2017 • OFF THE COB FESTIVAL MARKETPLACE

FOR MARINATED JACKFRUIT

1. Whisk soy sauce, sesame oil, garlic, ginger, and brown sugar in a small bowl until sugar dissolves.

2. Place jackfruit in a large bowl and cover with marinade. Refrigerate for at least 3 hours or overnight.

FOR "PICKLED" DE GALLO

Whisk water, vinegar, salt, and sugar in a small bowl until sugar dissolves. Add radish, carrot, jalapeño pepper, and cilantro. Cover and refrigerate at least 1 hour.

FOR CILANTRO CREMA

1. Preheat broiler to high. Place jalapeño pepper on baking sheet and broil, turning every 2 minutes, until pepper begins to blister. Place in a zip-top bag for 5 minutes. Remove skin and seeds, then finely chop.

2. Combine jalapeño pepper, sour cream, cilantro, and lime juice in a small bowl. Mix with an immersion blender until smooth and light green in color. Refrigerate until ready to serve.

MARINATED JACKFRUIT

½ cup soy sauce

½ cup sesame oil

5 cloves garlic, chopped

1 tablespoon chopped ginger

½ cup brown sugar

1 pound frozen jackfruit, thawed

"PICKLED" DE GALLO

½ cup water

2 tablespoons white vinegar

1 tablespoon salt

¼ cup sugar

⅔ cup shredded daikon radish

⅓ cup shredded carrot

½ jalapeño pepper, seeded and thinly sliced

1 tablespoon finely chopped fresh cilantro

CILANTRO CREMA

1 jalapeño pepper

½ cup sour cream

1 bunch fresh cilantro, finely chopped

Juice of 1 lime

TO SERVE

1. Drain Marinated Jackfruit. Place jackfruit in a medium-sized saucepan and cook over medium heat for 8 minutes, until it reaches a temperature of 165°F. Drain any excess juices. Drain "Pickled" de Gallo.

2. Place tortilla chips on a large platter. Top with jackfruit and pickled vegetables, and drizzle Cilantro Crema over it. Top with cilantro.

FOR SERVING

Marinated Jackfruit

"Pickled" de Gallo

1 (13-ounce) bag tortilla chips

Finely chopped fresh cilantro, to taste

Cilantro Crema

CHILE RELLENO EMPANADA WITH ÁRBOL SALSA

A guest favorite at the festival, the flaky, crispy empanada is a fun take on the Mexican classic—lots of cheese, roasted poblanos, and a little kick from the Árbol Salsa. If you can't find Oaxaca cheese, asadero or Monterey Jack can be substituted.

SERVES 4

INTRODUCED 2022 • PEPPERS CALI-ENTE FESTIVAL MARKETPLACE

ÁRBOL SALSA

2 árbol chiles

1 Roma tomato

¼ Spanish onion

2 garlic cloves

¼ cup canned roasted red peppers

1 tablespoon sherry vinegar

¼ cup canola oil

Coarse salt, to taste

FOR ÁRBOL SALSA

1 Place árbol chiles in a medium-sized glass bowl. Cover with boiling water and let rest for 15 minutes, until chiles are rehydrated. Drain water and remove stems.

2 Preheat oven to 425°F. Place árbol chiles, tomato, Spanish onion, and garlic on a small baking sheet. Roast for 5 to 7 minutes, until vegetables are soft and begin to char. Cool for 10 minutes.

3 Place roasted vegetables, roasted red peppers, sherry vinegar, and canola oil in a food processor or blender and blend until smooth. Season with salt, to taste. Set aside until ready to serve.

OPPOSITE: For the 2022 Disney California Adventure Food & Wine Festival, guests could enjoy various music acts taking to the Palisades Stage along Paradise Bay (top left) along with off-the-beaten-path table areas, such as those set up at the Sonoma Terrace Beer Garden (bottom left).

FOR EMPANADAS

1. Mix shredded mozzarella cheese, Oaxaca cheese, and diced roasted green peppers in a medium-sized bowl.

2. Place 3 tablespoons of the cheese filling in the center of each dough circle. Whisk egg and water in a small bowl. Brush egg mixture on the outer edge of the dough. Fold together to make a half-moon shape. Seal with fork or crimping tool.

3. With caution, preheat oil in Dutch oven or deep fryer to 375°F. Carefully fry empanadas, working in batches if necessary, for 3 to 4 minutes, until golden brown. Drain on paper towels.

TO SERVE

Top with crumbled cotija cheese, micro cilantro, and Árbol Salsa.

EMPANADAS

1 cup shredded mozzarella cheese

1 cup shredded Oaxaca cheese

1 cup canned diced roasted green peppers, drained

12 (5-inch) empanada dough circles (found in local grocery stores)

1 egg, beaten

1 tablespoon water

Oil, for frying

TOPPINGS

½ cup cotija cheese

¼ cup finely chopped fresh micro cilantro

Árbol Salsa

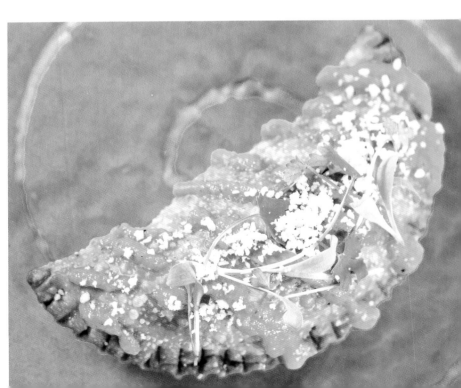

BRAISED WAGYU BEEF ON CREAMY POLENTA WITH HARICOT VERT AND RED ONION SALAD

You can braise these ribs a day ahead, and they are even better reheated with the stock. You can make the haricot vert salad ahead, too; then all that's last minute is the polenta.

SERVES 4

INTRODUCED 2017 • THE ONION LAIR FESTIVAL MARKETPLACE

FOR BRAISED WAGYU BEEF

1. Season ribs with salt and add to stock in a large pot. Bring to a boil, then reduce to simmer for 2½ to 3 hours, or until tender.

2. Remove beef from stock. Then cool and shred, adding a little stock for moisture. Season with salt and pepper.

3. Beef may be refrigerated, then reheated when ready to serve; make sure there is enough stock to keep beef moist.

FOR CREAMY POLENTA

1. Bring water to a boil in a heavy saucepan. Crush garlic cloves but keep each in one piece. Add garlic and thyme to boiling water for 60 seconds, then remove.

2. Slowly whisk polenta into boiling water over medium heat and whisk for 2 minutes. Reduce heat to low and cover pan. Cook at a simmer, stirring about every 10 minutes, for about 30 to 40 minutes.

3. Remove from heat and whisk in butter, then cheese. Season with salt. Serve warm.

BRAISED WAGYU BEEF

1½ pounds Wagyu chuck beef short ribs

Coarse salt, to taste

4 cups beef stock

Freshly ground black pepper, to taste

CREAMY POLENTA

4 cups water

4 cloves garlic

4 sprigs fresh thyme

1 cup polenta

½ cup unsalted butter

½ cup shredded Parmesan cheese

Coarse salt, to taste

FOR SALAD

1. Clean and blanch haricots verts in large pot of salted boiling water for 2 minutes. Remove from heat, immediately drain, and immerse in a bowl of ice water.

2. Mix garlic, shallot, and red wine vinegar in a serving bowl. Whisk in canola oil. Season with salt and pepper.

3. Drain the haricots verts and toss in dressing. Add the red onions to the salad and toss.

TO SERVE

Place a scoop of warm Creamy Polenta in center of plate. Top with Braised Wagyu Beef and Salad.

SALAD

½ pound fresh haricots verts (aka French green beans)

1 small clove garlic, peeled

1 shallot, finely chopped

2 tablespoons red wine vinegar

6 tablespoons canola oil

Coarse salt and freshly ground black pepper, to taste

½ small red onion, halved and finely sliced

BOTTOM: Chip 'n' Dale and the Jammin' Chefs (executive chef Mac-a-roni and master chefs Frank Beans, Sloppy Joe, and Rag-a-Tony) liven up the party at the 2018 Disney California Adventure Food & Wine Festival.

FRIED ARTICHOKE WITH CARBONARA GARLIC AÏOLI

Canned or jarred artichoke hearts work well, with bacon and garlic aïoli as the "carbonara" inspiration. Delicious with a crisp lager like a pilsner that showcases fruity aromas and spicy flavors.

SERVES 4

INTRODUCED 2017 • I ♥ ARTICHOKES FESTIVAL MARKETPLACE

FOR GARLIC AÏOLI

1. Place all ingredients except olive oil in bottom of a wide-mouth jar. Slowly pour oil over top so it remains separate.

2. Insert an immersion blender to rest at very bottom of jar. Without moving it, turn bender on high. Slowly raise immersion blender until ingredients emulsify. Set aside.

FOR FRIED ARTICHOKES

1. Pour vegetable oil to a depth of 2 inches in a deep sauté pan. With caution heat over medium heat to 350°F.

2. Dredge artichokes in seasoned coating mix, shaking off excess.

3. Working in batches, carefully lower coated artichokes into oil and fry until crisp, about 3 minutes. Remove with a slotted spoon and place on a plate lined with paper towels.

4. Place Parmesan, bacon, parsley, garlic, red pepper flakes, and pepper in a large bowl. Add fried artichokes and toss gently. Serve with Garlic Aïoli.

GARLIC AÏOLI

2 pasteurized egg yolks

1 tablespoon fresh lemon juice

½ tablespoon red wine vinegar

1 teaspoon Dijon mustard

1 teaspoon coarse salt

1 teaspoon sugar

1 clove garlic

1 cup light olive oil

FRIED ARTICHOKES

Vegetable oil, for frying

16-ounce can quartered artichoke hearts, drained

5-ounce box seasoned coating mix for frying

½ cup grated Parmesan cheese

¼ pound bacon, cooked and crumbled

2 tablespoons coarsely chopped Italian parsley

1 clove garlic, minced

1 teaspoon crushed red pepper flakes

1 teaspoon freshly ground black pepper

TORTA DE CHILAQUILES

Grab a knife and fork for this plant-based sandwich with all the messy goodness of chilaquiles. Soy-based sausage mixes with pinto beans for a vegetarian take on a classic.

SERVES 4

INTRODUCED 2023 • PARADISE GARDEN GRILL FESTIVAL MARKETPLACE

PICKLED RED ONIONS

1 medium red onion

½ cup red wine vinegar

½ cup lime juice

1½ teaspoons salt

CHILAQUILES

8 (6-inch) corn tortillas, cut into 8 triangles

Canola oil, for frying

Coarse salt, to taste

8 tomatillos

1 medium white onion

1 jalapeño pepper

2 serrano peppers

2 cloves garlic, peeled

1 bunch of cilantro leaves

FOR PICKLED RED ONIONS

Thinly slice onion and set aside. In a medium-sized bowl, combine red wine vinegar, lime juice, and salt. Add onions and stir to combine. Let rest for 20 to 30 minutes.

FOR CHILAQUILES

1   With caution, heat 1 to 2 inches of canola oil in a Dutch oven. Carefully fry triangles for 1 to 2 minutes, until golden brown. Remove and drain on paper towels. Add salt. Set aside.

2   Preheat oven to 425°F. Remove husks from tomatillos and wash. Cut onion into quarters. Remove stems and seeds from jalapeño and serrano peppers.

3   Place tomatillos, onions, jalapeño pepper, serrano peppers, and garlic cloves on a baking sheet. Roast for 15 to 20 minutes, stirring once until tomatillos and onions are charred. Cool for 10 to 15 minutes.

4   Pour in blender or food processor and blend until smooth. Add cilantro leaves and purée for 10 seconds.

5   Combine tortilla chips and tomatillo sauce in a large saucepan. Cook on low heat for 20 minutes, until chips are soft. Keep warm until ready to serve.

FOR SOY CHORIZO BEANS

1 Heat canola oil in a large skillet over medium heat for 5 minutes, until hot. Add soy chorizo and cook for 5 to 7 minutes, or until fully cooked.

2 Add cumin and garlic. Cook, stirring constantly for 1 minute, until fragrant. Add beans and liquid from can. Cook for 5 minutes until warm. Season with salt.

3 Purée bean mix until desired consistency. Keep warm until ready to serve.

FOR CHIPOTLE CREMA

Combine all ingredients in a medium-sized. Refrigerate until ready to serve.

FOR AVOCADO PULP

Remove seed from avocado and scoop pulp into small bowl. Mash until smooth. Add lime juice and salt. Set aside until ready to serve.

TO SERVE

1 Slice telera bread in half, leaving the last ½ inch of the bread attached. Heat a large skillet over medium heat for 5 minutes, until hot. Toast the inside of each telera for 2 minutes, or until golden brown.

2 Spread reserved Soy Chorizo Beans on bottom of bread. Top with Chilaquiles, Chipotle Crema, Pickled Red Onions, and cilantro. Top with Avocado Pulp.

SOY CHORIZO BEANS

2 tablespoons canola oil

8 ounces soy-based chorizo sausage

1 tablespoon ground cumin

1½ teaspoons minced garlic

15½-ounce can pinto beans

½ teaspoon salt

CHIPOTLE CREMA

1 cup plant-based sour cream

¼ cup chipotle purée

Coarse salt, to taste

AVOCADO PULP

2 medium ripe avocados

2 tablespoons fresh lime juice

½ teaspoon coarse salt

TORTA DE CHILAQUILES

4 telera (torta) rolls

¼ cup cilantro leaves

FRENCH ONION MAC & CHEESE

In this sophisticated version of a childhood favorite, buttery panko adds a nice crunchy topping. With sweet maltiness, a brown ale pairs perfectly.

SERVES 8

INTRODUCED 2017 • THE ONION LAIR FESTIVAL MARKETPLACE

¾ cup unsalted butter, divided

2 large white onions, thinly sliced

1 cup beef stock

2 tablespoons Worcestershire sauce

1 pound elbow macaroni

½ cup all-purpose flour

4 cups milk, whole or 2%

4 cups shredded Gruyère cheese

2 cups shredded sharp white Cheddar cheese

1 teaspoon coarse salt

½ teaspoon freshly ground black pepper

½ cup panko breadcrumbs

1 Preheat oven to 375°F. Spray a 3-quart baking dish with nonstick spray; set aside.

2 Melt ¼ cup butter in a large sauté pan over medium heat. Add onions and cook, stirring frequently until softened, about 5 minutes. Then add beef stock and Worcestershire sauce. Continue cooking until onions are very soft, liquids have been absorbed, and mixture is deep golden brown.

3 Meanwhile, cook macaroni according to package directions. Drain and set aside.

4 Melt 6 tablespoons butter in a large saucepan over medium heat. Whisk in flour until mixture is smooth and no lumps remain. Continue whisking slowly 2 minutes more. Slowly whisk in milk until smooth.

5 Remove from heat and add both cheeses, a handful at a time, stirring to completely melt. Stir in salt and pepper.

6 Combine cooked macaroni, onion mixture, and cheese sauce in a large bowl and stir to combine. Pour mixture into prepared baking dish.

7 Melt remaining 2 tablespoons butter in a small skillet. Remove from heat and toss panko in melted butter.

8 Top macaroni and cheese with panko mixture. Bake 30 minutes or until cheese is bubbling and topping is golden brown.

OPPOSITE, BOTTOM: The nighttime spectacular shows of Paradise Bay, such as the dancing waters shown here from 2012, are a hallmark to ending a day at the Disney California Adventure Food & Wine Festival.

ROASTED CAULIFLOWER, MEYER LEMON YOGURT, SUN-DRIED TOMATOES, AND CAPERS

MAINS & SIDES

The combination of roasted cauliflower and sun-dried tomatoes with crispy capers and a sweet-tart yogurt makes the perfect bite. Make the yogurt purée while the cauliflower is roasting, but fry the capers last minute to keep them crisp.

SERVES 8

INTRODUCED 2017 • LEMON GROVE FESTIVAL MARKETPLACE

ROASTED CAULIFLOWER

2 pounds cauliflower, divided

3 tablespoons vegetable oil

1 teaspoon coarse salt

MEYER LEMON YOGURT

1 whole Meyer lemon, washed

1 tablespoon sugar

2 teaspoons coarse salt

1 cup cauliflower pieces (reserved from Roasted Cauliflower)

10½ ounces Greek nonfat yogurt

FOR ROASTED CAULIFLOWER

1 Preheat oven to 400°F. Trim away leaves and stem from cauliflower and cut into bite-size florets, reserving all "crumbs" and smaller pieces (1 cup) for the purée within the Meyer Lemon Yogurt.

2 Toss florets with vegetable oil and season with salt. Place on baking sheet.

3 Bake for 10 to 15 minutes or until edges are brown and crispy. Keep room temperate until ready to serve.

FOR MEYER LEMON YOGURT

1. Slice lemon, remove all seeds, and finely chop. Place in a small bowl and add sugar and salt. Stir to combine and set aside at least 1 hour at room temperature. Then cover and refrigerate until ready to use. (It can be made up to 3 days in advance.)

2. Place reserved cauliflower trimmings in a small saucepan and add water to cover. Cook until very tender, about 5 minutes. Drain well and set aside in strainer until dry and cool enough to handle.

3. Place cooked cauliflower in a food processor and process until totally smooth. Fold cauliflower purée and lemon relish into yogurt. Set aside.

FOR FRIED CAPERS

1. Add vegetable oil in a large, deep skillet over medium-high heat. With caution, heat to 350°F. Pat capers with a paper towel until very dry.

2. Place a single caper in hot oil to test. It should sizzle gently. If oil is ready, add capers. Carefully fry, about 2 minutes. Remove and transfer to a plate lined with paper towels to drain.

TO SERVE

Place a spoonful of Meyer Lemon Yogurt on the bottom of a small serving plate. Top with Roasted Cauliflower and then with Fried Capers, sun-dried tomatoes, and chives.

FRIED CAPERS

Vegetable oil, for frying

2 tablespoons capers, drained

TOPPINGS

8 sun-dried tomato halves, chopped

¼ cup chopped chives

PEANUT BUTTER AND JELLY MAC

To a kid, it's the perfect combo. Adults are harder to convince, but once you try this peanut butter sauce on pasta, it's hard to resist. Delicious just with a drizzle of jelly, but the strawberry crumble topping is a nice finishing touch (or just skip it and dig in).

SERVES 4-6

INTRODUCED 2022 • NUTS ABOUT CHEESE FESTIVAL MARKETPLACE

FOR MACARONI

Cook macaroni according to package instructions. Drain and toss with canola oil to prevent sticking. Set aside.

FOR STRAWBERRY CRUMBLE

1. Preheat oven to 350°F. Line a baking sheet with parchment paper; set aside.

2. Combine flour, brown sugar and salt in the bowl of an electric mixer fitted with a paddle attachment on low speed until combined.

3. Add melted butter and strawberry jelly and mix on medium speed until crumbly.

4. Place on reserved sheet pan and bake for 6 to 8 minutes, until crumble begins to brown. Set aside.

FOR STRAWBERRY SAUCE

Heat strawberry jelly in a medium-sized saucepan over low heat for 5 minutes, until jelly is easily poured. Keep warm until ready to serve.

MACARONI

1 pound dried elbow macaroni

1 tablespoon canola oil

STRAWBERRY CRUMBLE

1 cup flour

½ cup brown sugar

⅛ teaspoon salt

¼ cup unsalted butter, melted

3 tablespoons strawberry jelly

STRAWBERRY SAUCE

½ cup strawberry jelly

FOR PEANUT BUTTER SAUCE

Melt butter in a large saucepan over medium heat. Add flour, and whisk for 2 minutes. Then add heavy cream, and stir constantly. When mixture reaches 175°F, remove from heat, and stir in peanut butter. Season with salt, to taste. Keep warm until ready to serve.

TO SERVE

Stir Macaroni into Peanut Butter Sauce. Evenly divide among 4 to 6 plates and top with Strawberry Crumble and Strawberry Sauce. Sprinkle strawberry-flavored popping candies on top.

PEANUT BUTTER SAUCE

2 tablespoons unsalted butter

¼ cup all-purpose flour

4 cups heavy cream

¾ cup creamy peanut butter

Coase salt, to taste

TOPPING

1 packet strawberry-flavored popping candies

WATERMELON-CUCUMBER POKE WITH CITRUS SOY AND TOGARASHI

MAINS & SIDES

A vegetarian version of tuna poke with crisp, sweet watermelon standing in for the fish.

SERVES 4

INTRODUCED 2019 • ONE IN A MELON FESTIVAL MARKETPLACE

FOR COMPRESSED WATERMELON

Place diced watermelon in vacuum sealer bag. Seal and remove air. Refrigerate for 8 hours.

FOR POKE SAUCE

Whisk soy sauce, water, sesame oil, and lime juice in a small bowl until combined. Refrigerate until ready to serve.

FOR CUCUMBER AND ONION MIX

Place cucumbers and onions in a small bowl. Season with togarashi pepper. Set aside.

FOR WATERMELON-CUCUMBER POKE

Drain Compressed Watermelon and toss in Poke Sauce. Evenly divide rice among 4 bowls. Top with Compressed Watermelon, Cucumber and Onion Mix, furikake, and fried shallots.

COMPRESSED WATERMELON

2 cups diced watermelon

POKE SAUCE

1 tablespoon soy sauce

2 teaspoons water

½ teaspoon sesame oil

½ teaspoon lime juice

CUCUMBER AND ONION MIX

⅓ cup diced cucumber

¼ cup diced red onion

¼ teaspoon togarashi pepper, plus more to taste

WATERMELON-CUCUMBER POKE

Compressed Watermelon

Poke Sauce

2 cups steamed white rice, cooled

Cucumber and Onion Mix

1 teaspoon furikake

¼ cup fried shallots

CHERRY LEMONADE WITH CHERRY PEARLS

Cherry popping pearls add a sweet, chewy element to this nonalcoholic beverage. You can find the little bursting balls in specialty stores or online.

SERVES 1

INTRODUCED 2017 • LEMON GROVE FESTIVAL MARKETPLACE

7 ounces lemonade

½ ounce cherry beverage syrup

2 ounces cherry popping pearls, divided

Ice cubes

Boba straw

In a mixing glass, stir together lemonade and cherry beverage syrup. Then place a third of the popping pearls in a clean serving glass and add lemonade-cherry mixture and another third of popping pearls. Add ice and remaining popping pearls. Serve with a boba straw.

MEYER LEMON GINGER MULE

A California take on a cocktail hour favorite with a splash of Meyer lemon instead of lime.

SERVES 1

INTRODUCED 2017 • LEMON GROVE FESTIVAL MARKETPLACE

1¼ ounces Meyer Lemon & Ginger Liqueur

½ ounce fresh lemon juice

4 ounces ginger beer

Crushed ice

Pour liqueur and lemon juice into a 16-ounce copper mug; stir in ginger beer and add crushed ice.

SUMMER BERRY PUDDING

SWEET ENDINGS & DESSERTS

So many layers of flavor! Make this a couple of days ahead so that the brioche can soak up all the berry juice. And there's no baking!

SERVES 8

INTRODUCED 2020 • BERRY PATCH FESTIVAL MARKETPLACE

FOR BERRY FILLING

Combine blueberries, red currants, raspberries, orange liqueur, and sugar in a large bowl. Stir gently. Set aside for 15 minutes, or for up to 4 hours.

FOR YOGURT TOPPING

Place whipping cream, sugar, and vanilla bean paste in the bowl of an electric mixer fitted with a whisk attachment. Whip until medium peaks form. Then fold in yogurt and refrigerate until ready to use.

FOR SUMMER BERRY PUDDING

1. Line an 8-inch springform pan with plastic wrap. Then slice brioche into 1-inch-thick slices. Line bottom of prepared springform pan with sliced bread.

2. Using a slotted spoon, fill center of the bread with berries. Make sure to save juices from the berries in the bowl. Top with remaining bread slices.

3. Pour reserved juices on top of bread and cover with plastic wrap. Refrigerate for 1 to 2 days.

TO SERVE

Place a plate on top of the springform pan and carefully invert pan. Release pan sides and remove plastic wrap. Serve with Yogurt Topping and fresh berries. Garnish with mint.

BERRY FILLING

2 cups fresh blueberries

2 cups fresh or frozen red currants

4 cups fresh raspberries

3 tablespoons orange liqueur

½ cup sugar

YOGURT TOPPING

1 cup heavy whipping cream

1 tablespoon sugar

1 teaspoon vanilla bean paste (or vanilla extract)

¼ cup Greek yogurt

SUMMER BERRY PUDDING

1 (1-pound) loaf brioche

Berry Filling

Yogurt Topping

½ cup fresh berries

Mint sprig, optional

OPPOSITE, BOTTOM: Awaiting its next musical act, the colorful Palisades Stage shines bright in the sun at the 2022 Disney California Adventure Food & Wine Festival.

CELEBRATION CHOCOLATE FUDGE BROWNIE

The warm chocolate glaze on this fudge cake takes it over the top. If you prefer, use a fluted tube pan (about 9-inch round) instead of mini fluted tube pans and bake for 45 to 50 minutes.

SERVES 15

INTRODUCED 2023 • UNCORK CALIFORNIA FESTIVAL MARKETPLACE

GOOEY FUDGE CAKE

1¾ cups sugar

1¾ cups unsalted butter, softened

6 eggs

2 cups powdered sugar

2¼ cups all-purpose flour

¾ cup unsweetened cocoa powder

2 cups chopped pecans

FOR GOOEY FUDGE CAKE

1. Preheat oven to 325°F. Grease and flour 15 mini fluted tube pans (each 4-inch round). Set aside.

2. Cream sugar and butter in the bowl of an electric mixer fitted with a paddle attachment until fluffy. Add eggs, one at a time, until fully incorporated. Add powdered sugar, ½ cup at a time, and mix on low speed until combined.

3. Whisk all-purpose flour and cocoa powder together in a small bowl. Gradually add to sugar mix and blend on low speed until mixed. Add pecans and fold until just combined. Do not overmix.

4. Fill prepared pans two-thirds full with batter. Bake for 20 to 25 minutes, until top is set but center is still soft. Cool completely before removing from pan.

ABOVE: The nightly glow from Pixar Pier and all along Paradise Bay, such as the view shown here from 2020, sets the mood for Disney California Adventure Food & Wine Festival feasting.

FOR CHOCOLATE PECAN GLAZE

Heat butter and milk in small saucepan over medium heat until butter is melted. Remove from heat. Then whisk in cocoa powder and powdered sugar until smooth. Stir in pecans. Keep warm until ready to serve.

TO SERVE

Remove cakes from molds. Top each cake with warm Chocolate Pecan Glaze, white chocolate crunch pearls, and edible glitter stars, if using.

CHOCOLATE PECAN GLAZE

½ cup unsalted butter

6 tablespoons milk

¼ cup cocoa powder

1 cup powdered sugar

1 cup chopped pecans

TOPPING

White chocolate crunch pearls, optional

Edible glitter stars, optional

MAPLE-BACON WHOOPIE PIE

Maple cream cheese and apple pie filling are sandwiched between cake-like bacon-flavored cookies, with a crunch of bacon brittle on top. Baking pans lined with parchment paper can be used instead of whoopie pie mats; use a 2-tablespoon scoop and make 12 round cakes on each baking pan, leaving 2 inches between each. (If you are not using whoopie pie mats, reduce the water in the cake by ¼ cup.)

MAKES 12

INTRODUCED 2017 • BACON TWIST FESTIVAL MARKETPLACE

BACON BRITTLE

2 tablespoons unsalted butter

¼ cup sugar

2 tablespoons chopped cooked bacon

BACON CAKE CIRCLES

1 box white cake mix plus ingredients called for on box

¼ cup chopped cooked bacon

FOR BACON BRITTLE

1 Place silicone baking mat on baking pan.

2 Melt butter in a small saucepan over medium heat. Stir in sugar. Continue cooking over medium heat for 3 to 4 minutes, until sugar and butter mixture is golden brown. Then remove from heat and stir in bacon.

3 Carefully pour mixture on top of silicone baking mat and spread evenly. Cool for 45 minutes, or until completely cool. Break into 12 small pieces. Set aside.

FOR BACON CAKE CIRCLES

1 Preheat oven to 350°F. Line 2 half-sheet pans with whoopie pie mats.

2 Prepare cake mix according to package directions. Once all ingredients are combined, gently stir in bacon.

3 Fill whoopie pie mats with cake batter. Bake 15 to 20 minutes, until cake springs back when lightly touched. Cool completely.

FOR MAPLE CREAM CHEESE ICING

1. Place egg whites in the bowl of an electric mixer fitted with a whisk attachment. Whip on medium speed until egg whites form soft peaks. Set aside.

2. Place sugar in a small saucepan. Slowly add water. Stir gently until mixed. Cook over medium heat without stirring for 4 to 5 minutes, or until mixture reaches 242.6°F. Remove from heat.

3. Turn mixer to medium speed and whip egg whites until soft peaks return.

4. Slowly pour hot sugar into egg whites, making sure to pour along side of bowl.

5. Continue beating for 5 minutes, until bottom of mixing bowl is cool and egg whites are shiny.

6. Add butter to egg whites in 3 separate batches. Increase mixer speed to high. Mix for 4 to 6 minutes, until shiny and smooth. Then add vanilla extract and mix for 30 seconds.

7. Place cream cheese in a separate mixing bowl of an electric mixer fitted with a paddle attachment. Beat on medium speed for 2 to 3 minutes, until very smooth.

8. Add egg white–butter mixture to cream cheese and beat on medium speed for 3 minutes, until combined. Add maple syrup and combine on low speed for 30 seconds. Set aside until ready to use.

FOR WHOOPIE PIES

1. Place icing in piping bag fitted with large round tip. Pipe a large ring of icing on flat side of 12 of the Bacon Cake Circles. Leave center of each circle open.

2. Spoon 2 tablespoons of apple pie filling into center of each circle. Top with remaining cake circles and press gently. Add one piece of Bacon Brittle to each whoopie pie before serving.

MAPLE CREAM CHEESE ICING

2 large egg whites

½ cup sugar

2 tablespoons water

¾ cup unsalted butter, room temperature, divided

½ teaspoon pure vanilla extract

½ cup cream cheese, room temperature

1 tablespoon maple syrup

WHOOPIE PIES

Maple Cream Cheese Icing

24 Bacon Cake Circles

1 (21-ounce) can apple pie filling

12 pieces Bacon Brittle

VANILLA BEAN CRÈME FRAÎCHE PANNA COTTA WITH LEMON MADELEINES

The lemon madeleines are the perfect accompaniment to the creamy panna cotta. You can find Italian Amarena cherries in specialty shops or online. Sip with a moscato for a sweet ending.

SERVES 6

INTRODUCED 2017 • OLIVE US FESTIVAL MARKETPLACE

CRÈME FRAÎCHE PANNA COTTA

2 teaspoons powdered gelatin

¼ cup cold water

½ vanilla bean, split down middle

1 cup plus 2 tablespoons whole milk

1 cup plus 2 tablespoons heavy cream

¼ cup sugar

½ cup plus 2 tablespoons crème fraîche

FOR CRÈME FRAÎCHE PANNA COTTA

1. Place gelatin in a small bowl and add cold water. Stir and set aside. Then scrape seeds from vanilla bean with sharp knife, and set aside.

2. Heat milk, heavy cream, and sugar in a medium-sized saucepan over low heat until mixture starts to steam. Do not boil.

3. Add vanilla bean and seeds to milk. Let steam for about 1 minute. Then remove from heat and add gelatin. Stir to dissolve and set aside to cool.

4. Once mixture cools, whisk in crème fraîche. Then pour mixture through mesh strainer to remove any lumps and vanilla bean pieces.

5. Pour panna cotta into 6 (½-cup) ramekins, leaving about ¼ inch on top. Cover each ramekin with plastic wrap and refrigerate until firm, about 3 to 4 hours.

FOR LEMON OLIVE OIL MADELEINES

1. Preheat oven to 350°F. Whisk eggs and sugar in a small mixing bowl until pale and fluffy.

2. Whisk olive oil, lemon juice, lemon zest, and vanilla extract in a separate bowl. Add egg to mixture, whisking thoroughly, and then set aside.

3. Combine flour, baking powder, and salt in a medium-sized bowl. Add wet ingredients and fold together, breaking down any lumps.

4. Prepare baking sheets with cooking spray. Pour 1 tablespoon batter into mini-madeleine mold. Bake for about 6 to 8 minutes until golden brown. Set aside to cool. Repeat until all batter has been used.

TO SERVE

Remove panna cotta from refrigerator. Spread 1 to 2 teaspoons of Amarena cherries in syrup on each serving. Dip one madeleine into side of each ramekin. Serve with additional madeleines on small plates.

LEMON OLIVE OIL MADELEINES

4 large eggs

1 cup sugar

½ cup lemon olive oil

½ cup lemon juice

1½ teaspoons lemon zest

1½ teaspoons vanilla extract

1 cup all-purpose flour

1½ teaspoons baking powder

½ teaspoon salt

FOR SERVING

Amarena cherries in syrup

CHAPTER THREE
EPCOT INTERNATIONAL FLOWER & GARDEN FESTIVAL
at the Walt Disney World Resort

THE GRANDDADDY OF EPCOT festivals, the EPCOT International Flower & Garden Festival, debuted in 1994, a showcase for the brilliant Disney topiaries and other floral wonders. Food wasn't part of the inaugural festival, but Outdoor Kitchens were added over the years, with mini gardens showcasing the plants used to make the dishes. This is one festival where the fabulous Disney foliage shares top billing with the food.

THESE PAGES: Decorative flower beds and Disney character topiaries are focal points of the annual EPCOT International Flower & Garden Festival, including this display of characters from the 1994 classic *The Lion King* (previous pages, 2021). The 2023 festival (above and opposite) featured Mirabel from *Encanto* (2021) and Tiana from *The Princess and the Frog* (2009).

HONEY TANDOORI CHICKEN FLATBREAD

Start this recipe a day ahead so vegetables and tandoori chicken can marinate for 24 hours. Once you've got those in the fridge, the rest easily comes together with store-bought naan. Don't skip the drizzle of honey sour cream—it's a delightful finish.

SERVES 6

INTRODUCED 2018 • HONEY BEE-STRO OUTDOOR KITCHEN

FOR MARINATED VEGETABLES

1 Preheat oven to 350°F. Toss onions and garlic in 1 tablespoon canola oil, ⅛ teaspoon salt, and ⅛ teaspoon pepper. Arrange on a baking sheet.

2 Cook for 30 minutes, stirring every 10 minutes, until onions begin to caramelize. Cool for 20 minutes.

3 Drain bell peppers and cut into 1-inch pieces. Place garlic, onions, and bell peppers in medium-sized bowl. Add rosemary and thyme, plus remaining oil, salt, and pepper. Marinate in the refrigerator for at least 24 hours.

MARINATED VEGETABLES

½ cup roughly chopped white onion

2 garlic cloves

½ cup canola oil, divided

½ teaspoon coarse salt, divided

½ teaspoon freshly ground black pepper, divided

1 (12-ounce) jar roasted red and yellow bell peppers

1 sprig rosemary

1 sprig thyme

OPPOSITE, BOTTOM: An enclosed butterfly garden, like the one shown here from 2021, is a fan-favorite highlight of the EPCOT International Flower & Garden Festival.

(RECIPE CONTINUES ON PAGE 74)

HONEY TANDOORI CHICKEN FLATBREAD

(CONTINUED)

FOR TANDOORI CHICKEN

1. Combine all ingredients except chicken in a large bowl. Add chicken thighs and coat. Marinate in refrigerator for 24 hours.

2. Preheat oven to 350°F. Remove chicken from marinade and place on a baking sheet. Bake for 30 minutes, until chicken is fully cooked. Cut chicken into 1-inch cubes. Set aside until ready to use.

FOR ONION CREAM

1. Heat canola oil in a medium-sized skillet over medium heat for 5 minutes, until hot. Add onions, reduce heat to medium-low, and sauté for 8 minutes, until soft. Add heavy cream and cook for 3 minutes, until cream begins to bubble.

2. Remove from heat and cool for 10 minutes. Pour into blender and purée until smooth. Season with salt, to taste. Set aside.

TANDOORI CHICKEN

½ cup yogurt

2 tablespoons lemon juice

¼ cup canola oil

½ cup diced onion

3 tablespoons fresh minced ginger

1 tablespoon minced garlic

1 teaspoon chili-garlic sauce

2 teaspoons smoked paprika

1 tablespoon salt

1½ teaspoons ground cumin

1½ teaspoons ground turmeric

1½ teaspoons ground coriander

2 teaspoons ground cayenne pepper

¼ cup honey

1 pound boneless, skinless chicken thighs

ONION CREAM

1 tablespoon canola oil

½ white onion, cut into 1-inch pieces

½ cup heavy cream

Coarse salt, to taste

FOR HONEY SOUR CREAM

Mix honey and sour cream together in a small bowl. Refrigerate until ready to serve.

FOR HONEY TANDOORI CHICKEN FLATBREAD

Preheat oven to 350°F. Place naan on baking sheets. Smear 3 tablespoons of Onion Cream on each naan. Evenly divide cheese, Tandoori Chicken, and Marinated Vegetables among the naan. Bake for 7 minutes, until cheese is melted. Drizzle on Honey Sour Cream, and top with micro watercress.

BELOW: For the 2022 EPCOT International Flower & Garden Festival, guests could interact up close with butterflies in an enclosed butterfly garden.

HONEY SOUR CREAM

2 tablespoons honey

¼ cup sour cream

HONEY TANDOORI CHICKEN FLATBREAD

6 naan flatbreads

1⅛ cups Onion Cream, divided

2 cups grated white Cheddar cheese

Tandoori Chicken

Marinated Vegetables

Honey Sour Cream

Micro watercress

SMOKED SALMON TARTARE AND POTATO BISCUIT

You might make just the biscuits, or you might make just the salmon tartare—both are delicious stand-alones. But together they're a match made in heaven. Pair with a cava brut rosé.

SERVES 5

INTRODUCED 2014 • THE BUTTERCUP COTTAGE OUTDOOR KITCHEN

FOR POTATO BISCUITS

1. Cook potato in boiling salted water until very tender. Drain well, mash, and cool completely.

2. Preheat oven to 350°F. Combine flour, baking powder, salt, and baking soda in a bowl; cut in butter with a pastry blender or with two knives until mixture resembles coarse meal.

3. Stir in mashed potato, Cheddar cheese, buttermilk, and chives, just until moistened.

4. Turn dough out onto a floured surface and knead lightly until dough comes together. Roll dough to a 1-inch thickness, and cut with a 3-inch round cutter.

5. Place on a baking sheet. Combine beaten egg and water, and brush egg wash over biscuits. Sprinkle with salt. Bake 25 to 35 minutes, or until golden.

POTATO BISCUITS

1 large russet potato (about 14 ounces), peeled and diced

1½ cups all-purpose flour

2¼ teaspoons baking powder

1 teaspoon coarse salt

¾ teaspoon baking soda

¼ cup cold unsalted butter

1 cup shredded white Cheddar cheese

½ cup buttermilk

2 tablespoons chopped fresh chives

1 egg, beaten

2 teaspoons water

Coarse salt, to taste

FOR SMOKED SALMON TARTARE

1. Place raw salmon in freezer 20 minutes. Meanwhile, finely chop smoked salmon. Remove raw salmon from freezer and mince with a sharp knife. (Do not use a food processor or mixture will be mushy. Alternatively, run both kinds of salmon through the grinder attachment on an electric mixer.)

2. Combine smoked and raw salmon, capers, and shallot in a large bowl. Gently stir in lemon oil or lemon zest and dill. Add salt and pepper to taste.

TO SERVE

Slice a Potato Biscuit in half. Spoon 3 tablespoons Smoked Salmon Tartare over bottom half of biscuit. Top with ½ teaspoon sour cream and a dill frond. Place top half of biscuit slightly to the side, half covering tartare.

SMOKED SALMON TARTARE

1 cup (½-inch-diced) raw sushi-grade salmon, skinless

1 cup roughly chopped smoked salmon

2 tablespoons capers, very finely chopped

2 tablespoons minced shallot

1½ teaspoons pure lemon oil (or 2 teaspoons finely grated lemon zest)

1 tablespoon finely chopped fresh dill

Coarse salt and freshly ground black pepper, to taste

TOPPINGS

Sour cream

Dill fronds

IMPOSSIBLE™ ITALIAN SAUSAGE AND KALE SOUP

You add the spices to turn this plant-based ground sausage into an Italian-style sausage. If you can't find kale, spinach or collards work—and don't leave out the dollop of pesto on top. And the soup is even better the second day.

SERVES 6-8

INTRODUCED 2021 • TROWEL & TRELLIS OUTDOOR KITCHEN, HOSTED BY IMPOSSIBLE FOODS

FOR IMPOSSIBLE™ ITALIAN SAUSAGE

Combine all ingredients in a medium-sized bowl. Mix until seasonings are fully incorporated. Refrigerate until ready to use.

FOR IMPOSSIBLE™ ITALIAN SAUSAGE AND KALE SOUP

1. Heat olive oil in a large pot or Dutch oven over medium heat for 5 minutes, until hot. Add Impossible™ Italian Sausage mix and cook, stirring occasionally, for 8 to 10 minutes, until fully cooked.

2. Add onions, garlic, and crushed red pepper and cook for 5 minutes, until onions begin to soften. Add white wine and cook for 2 minutes, making sure to scrape any browned bits of sausage from the bottom.

3. Add potatoes, oregano, and vegetable broth. Bring to a boil, cover, and reduce to a simmer for 10 to 15 minutes, until potatoes are soft. Add dairy-free cooking cream and stir until incorporated.

IMPOSSIBLE™ ITALIAN SAUSAGE

1 (14-ounce) package Impossible™ Sausage Made From Plants (Ground)

2 tablespoons paprika

1 tablespoon fennel seed

1 tablespoon coarse salt

2 teaspoons dried oregano

2 teaspoons granulated garlic

1 tablespoon anise seed

1 teaspoon crushed red pepper

IMPOSSIBLE™ ITALIAN SAUSAGE AND KALE SOUP

1 tablespoon olive oil

Impossible™ Italian Sausage

1 medium onion, diced

3 cloves garlic, minced

½ teaspoon crushed red pepper

1 cup white wine

6 small red potatoes, diced

1 tablespoon chopped fresh oregano

6 cups vegetable broth

¾ cup dairy-free cooking cream

4 Combine water and cornstarch in a small bowl. Bring soup to a boil and slowly add cornstarch mix. Simmer for 5 minutes, stirring often, until soup is slightly thickened.

5 Add chopped kale and stir until wilted. Add sherry vinegar. Season with additional sherry vinegar, salt, and pepper, to taste.

TO SERVE

Ladle soup into bowls. Top each with 1 to 2 tablespoons of pesto and a toasted flatbread cracker.

2 tablespoons water

2 tablespoons cornstarch

1 bunch (½ pound) kale, chopped

¼ cup sherry vinegar, plus more to taste

Coarse salt and freshly ground black pepper, to taste

TOPPINGS

1 cup pesto

8 toasted flatbread crackers

ABOVE, TOP RIGHT: A topiary of a fairy-sized Tinker Bell was a delightful part of the 2023 EPCOT International Flower & Garden Festival.

ABOVE, BOTTOM RIGHT: For the 2013 EPCOT International Flower & Garden Festival, Lady and the Tramp topiaries welcomed guests to the Italy pavilion in World Showcase.

IMPOSSIBLE™ LUMPIA

STARTERS & SMALL PLATES

You might not know this traditional Filipino treat is plant based—the ginger, garlic, onions, and cilantro flavor the crispy fried rolls. Serve with your favorite sweet chili sauce.

SERVES 4

INTRODUCED 2023 • TROWEL & TRELLIS OUTDOOR KITCHEN, HOSTED BY IMPOSSIBLE FOODS

12 ounces Impossible™ Beef Made From Plants

½ cup shredded carrots

4 teaspoons tamari sauce

2 tablespoons minced garlic

1 tablespoon ginger purée

1 tablespoon diced white onion

1 teaspoon chopped cilantro

16 lumpia wrappers

Oil, for frying

Favorite sweet Thai chili sauce, for serving

1 Combine Impossible™ Beef, carrots, tamari sauce, garlic, ginger purée, and onions in a large bowl until well mixed.

2 Place one lumpia wrapper on cutting board. Place 2 tablespoons of filling in the center of wrapper.

3 Roll one edge of the wrapper toward the center. Fold in both sides and continue rolling. Moisten the edge with water to seal the lumpia. Repeat with remaining lumpia wrappers. (If you notice, the photo leaves the ends open, but we found that folding the edges makes it easier to handle at home.)

4 With caution, heat 1 inch of oil in frying pan to 350°F. Carefully place lumpia in frying pan and fry for 3 minutes on each side, until filling is 165°F inside and lumpia wrapper is golden brown. Drain on paper towels. Serve with sweet Thai chili sauce.

OPPOSITE, BOTTOM: A happy Figment topiary beckons guests walking toward the IMAGINATION! pavilion during the 2021 Taste of EPCOT International Flower & Garden Festival.

SMOKED BRISKET WITH CHORIZO-CHEESE FONDUE

If you start the brisket from scratch, you can use a smoker or roast in the oven. (But it's also a great use for leftover brisket.) For serving, put a ramekin of the chorizo-cheese sauce on the side for extra dipping.

SERVES 6

INTRODUCED 2019 • THE SMOKEHOUSE: BARBECUE AND BREWS OUTDOOR KITCHEN

FOR SMOKED BRISKET

1. Mix all dry ingredients together in a medium-sized bowl until fully combined. Generously rub brisket with dry rub, and wrap tightly in plastic wrap. Place in pan or container and refrigerate overnight.

2. Next day, remove plastic wrap and place brisket in smoker at 250°F for 8 hours or until internal temperature reaches 210°F. *If you prefer to roast in the oven, sprinkle liquid smoke over rubbed brisket and refrigerate overnight. Next day, loosely but completely wrap brisket in heavy-duty foil and place in a baking pan. Bake in a 230°F oven for 8 hours or until internal temperature reaches 210°F.*

3. Allow meat to rest for 10 minutes. Then shred brisket and keep warm with foil.

SMOKED BRISKET

½ cup brown sugar

¼ cup coarse salt

1½ tablespoons chili powder

1 tablespoon paprika

1 tablespoon onion powder

1 tablespoon garlic powder

1 tablespoon freshly ground black pepper

½ tablespoon ground coriander

½ tablespoon ground cumin

1 teaspoon dried oregano

2½ pounds beef brisket

1 tablespoon liquid smoke (if using oven preparation method)

OPPOSITE, BOTTOM: For the 2013 EPCOT International Flower & Garden Festival, topiaries of Snow White and her seven friends greeted guests to World Showcase.

(RECIPE CONTINUES ON PAGE 84)

SMOKED BRISKET WITH CHORIZO-CHEESE FONDUE

(CONTINUED)

FOR CHORIZO-CHEESE FONDUE

1 Cook chorizo, onions, and butter in a medium-sized pot over medium heat, being careful not to burn.

2 Add flour and stir constantly for 3 to 5 minutes to ensure the flour taste has been cooked out. Then add cream, salt, and pepper. Bring just to a simmer and reduce heat to low.

3 Simmer for 8 to 10 minutes, stirring occasionally until thickened and mixture coats the back of the spoon.

4 Add Tabasco® sauce, and stir to combine. Then add cheeses slowly, stirring until completely melted. Keep warm or reheat at serving time.

FOR GREEN TOMATO SALSA

Combine all ingredients in a small bowl. Let stand for at least 1 hour, allowing flavors to incorporate.

CHORIZO-CHEESE FONDUE

½ pound ground chorizo

¼ cup diced onion

1½ tablespoons unsalted butter

2 tablespoons all-purpose flour

2 cups heavy cream

¼ teaspoon salt

¼ teaspoon ground white pepper

¼ teaspoon Tabasco® sauce

8 ounces Monterey Jack cheese, grated

4 ounces Gruyère cheese, grated

GREEN TOMATO SALSA

1 green tomato, diced

¼ cup diced red onion

1 teaspoon minced serrano pepper

1 tablespoon finely chopped fresh cilantro

1 tablespoon fresh lime juice

1 teaspoon white vinegar

2 teaspoons olive oil

⅛ teaspoon salt

⅛ teaspoon freshly ground black pepper

FOR BARBECUE DRIZZLE

Combine all ingredients in a small bowl. Refrigerate for at least 1 hour, allowing flavors to incorporate.

FOR POTATO BOAT

1. Preheat oven to 400°F. Bake potatoes in oven until almost tender, approximately 60 minutes.

2. Cut potatoes in half lengthwise and scoop out half of the center, creating a boat shape. (Reserve potato pulp for other uses or recipes.)

3. Return potato boats to the oven and bake until golden brown, approximately 10 minutes.

TO SERVE

Place one Potato Boat on each plate. Generously fill each boat with shredded beef brisket. Top with ¼ cup Chorizo-Cheese Fondue, 2 to 3 tablespoons Green Tomato Salsa, and Barbecue Drizzle, to taste.

BARBECUE DRIZZLE

2 tablespoons of your favorite barbecue sauce

2 tablespoons mayonnaise

½ teaspoon of your favorite pickle juice

POTATO BOAT

3 large baking potatoes

BELOW: Dueling topiaries of Captain Hook and Peter Pan were a specialty of the United Kingdom pavilion during the 2021 Taste of EPCOT International Flower & Garden Festival.

BEEF BRISKET BURNT ENDS HASH

MAINS & SIDES

You'll need leftover beef brisket (or pick some up at your favorite local barbecue place!) to make this hearty hash topped with cheese fondue. The pickled jalapeños add a spicy crunch to counter the richness. Serve with a California Zinfandel.

SERVES 4-6

INTRODUCED 2016 • THE SMOKEHOUSE: BARBECUES AND BREWS OUTDOOR KITCHEN

FOR PICKLED JALAPEÑO PEPPERS

1 Place onions and jalapeño peppers in a medium-sized glass bowl.

2 Combine white vinegar, water, sugar, salt, black peppercorns, bay leaf, garlic, and coriander in a small saucepan. Cook over high heat until mixture boils.

3 Pour brine over onions and jalapeño peppers. Cover and refrigerate at least 24 hours.

FOR WHITE CHEDDAR CHEESE FONDUE

1 Melt butter in a medium-sized saucepan over medium heat. Add onions and sauté 5 to 8 minutes, or until onions are translucent.

2 Add flour, stirring constantly, for 3 to 5 minutes. Do not allow mixture to brown.

3 Add cream, salt, white pepper and nutmeg. Cook over medium heat, stirring constantly, 5 minutes, or until simmering. Reduce heat to low and simmer, stirring occasionally, 20 to 25 minutes, until mixture is thick and coats the back of a spoon.

PICKLED JALAPEÑO PEPPERS

½ cup thinly sliced white onion

1 cup sliced jalapeño peppers

1 cup white vinegar

¾ cup water

3 tablespoons sugar

1 tablespoon salt

1 tablespoon black peppercorns

1 dried bay leaf

1 clove garlic

1 teaspoon coriander seeds

WHITE CHEDDAR CHEESE FONDUE

1 tablespoon unsalted butter

¼ cup diced onion

1 tablespoon all-purpose flour

1½ cups heavy cream

¼ teaspoon salt

⅛ teaspoon ground white pepper

⅛ teaspoon ground nutmeg

⅛ teaspoon hot sauce

1 cup shredded aged white Cheddar cheese

½ cup shredded mozzarella cheese

2 tablespoons diced jalapeño pepper

4 Add hot sauce. Slowly add Cheddar cheese and mozzarella cheese, stirring constantly, 3 to 5 minutes, until cheese melts and is creamy.

5 Add diced jalapeño peppers. Keep warm until ready to serve.

FOR BURNT ENDS BRISKET HASH

1 Heat canola oil in a large sauté pan over medium heat for 5 minutes, or until oil is shimmering.

2 Carefully add potatoes. Cook potatoes over medium heat, stirring occasionally, 6 to 8 minutes, until potatoes are golden and cooked through.

3 Add remaining vegetables. Cook 3 to 5 minutes, until softened. Season with salt and pepper.

4 To serve, evenly divide Burnt Ends Brisket Hash among plates. Top with White Cheddar Cheese Fondue and Pickled Jalapeño Peppers.

BEEF BRISKET BURNT ENDS HASH

1 tablespoon canola oil

1 medium white potato, diced

½ cup diced white onion

¼ cup diced celery

¼ cup diced poblano peppers

2 tablespoons diced jalapeño peppers

3 cups cubed smoked beef brisket

½ teaspoon coarse salt

½ teaspoon freshly ground black pepper

CHICKEN-ANDOUILLE GUMBO WITH CAJUN RICE

MAINS & SIDES

There's a lot of prep for this classic Louisiana dish with a kick of spice, but once you start cooking, it comes together in under two hours. And you can always make it a day ahead to feed a crowd—it's an easy recipe to double.

SERVES 4

INTRODUCED 2022 • MAGNOLIA TERRACE OUTDOOR KITCHEN

FOR CHICKEN-ANDOUILLE GUMBO

1. Melt butter in a large skillet over medium heat until melted. Add flour and reduce heat to low. Whisk constantly for 15 to 20 minutes, until roux is dark brown in color. Remove pan from heat and set aside.

2. Heat stockpot or Dutch oven over medium heat for 5 minutes, until hot. Add sliced andouille and tasso. Cook for 8 minutes until meat begins to brown. Remove from skillet and set aside.

3. Return pot to stovetop, add 1 tablespoon olive oil, and heat for 5 minutes over medium heat. Add chicken thighs and cook for 8 minutes, until fully cooked. Remove from skillet.

4. Add remaining tablespoon oil to the stock pot. Sauté garlic, onions, celery, green pepper, oregano, thyme, cayenne, and Cajun seasoning for 5 to 8 minutes, until vegetables begin to soften.

5. Carefully add reserved roux to vegetables and stir until combined. Add chicken stock, Worcestershire sauce, and Tabasco® sauce. Bring to a boil, then reduce to simmer.

CHICKEN-ANDOUILLE GUMBO

½ cup unsalted butter

⅔ cup all-purpose flour

½ pound andouille sausage, sliced

½ pound tasso ham, diced

2 tablespoons olive oil, divided

1 pound boneless, skinless chicken thighs, cut into 2-inch pieces

2 cloves garlic, minced

1 cup diced onion

½ cup diced celery

½ cup diced green pepper

1½ teaspoons chopped fresh oregano

1½ teaspoons chopped fresh thyme

¼ teaspoon ground cayenne

1 tablespoon Cajun seasoning

2¾ cups chicken stock

2 tablespoons Worcestershire sauce

2 tablespoons Tabasco® sauce, plus more to taste

1 bay leaf

1 cup sliced frozen okra

6   Allow gumbo to simmer for 30 minutes, until reduced by a quarter. Add bay leaf, chicken, tasso, and andouille to skillet and simmer for 5 minutes, until heated through.

7   Turn off heat and stir in okra, tomatoes, and gumbo filé. Season with salt and pepper. Keep warm until ready to serve.

FOR CAJUN RICE

1   Place rice in strainer and rinse under cold water until water runs clear. Then bring water and salt to a boil in a medium-sized saucepan. Stir in rice, cover, and reduce heat to low.

2   Allow rice to cook for 15 to 18 minutes, until water is fully absorbed and rice is soft. Remove from heat.

3   Stir in butter and Cajun seasoning. Add additional salt and Tabasco® sauce, if desired. Keep warm until ready to serve.

TO SERVE

Serve Chicken-Andouille Gumbo with Cajun Rice. Top with green onions.

½ cup diced tomatoes

1 teaspoon gumbo filé

Coarse salt and freshly ground black pepper, to taste

CAJUN RICE

1½ cups long grain rice

2¼ cup water

1 tablespoon salt, plus more to taste

2 tablespoons unsalted butter

1½ tablespoons Cajun seasoning

Tabasco® sauce, to taste

TOPPING

⅔ cup sliced green onion

FRIED GREEN TOMATO-CRAB SALAD

MAINS & SIDES

The trio of crunchy tomatoes, cool crab, and a robust remoulade makes a delicious appetizer for any party.

SERVES 4

INTRODUCED 2019 • ARBOR AT GARDENERS TERRACE

FOR CRAB SALAD

Combine culantro, fennel, cilantro, garlic, canola oil, lime juice, serrano pepper, and green onions in a blender. Purée until smooth. Season with salt and pepper. Place crab meat in a medium-sized bowl. Pour puréed dressing on top. Then cover and refrigerate until ready to serve.

FOR REMOULADE

Combine mayonnaise, capers, whole-grain mustard, garlic, horseradish, lemon juice, shallots, and parsley in a small bowl. Season with salt and pepper, to taste. Then cover and refrigerate until ready to serve.

FOR PAPRIKA OIL

Warm canola oil in a small saucepan over medium heat until it reaches 180°F. Remove from heat and add smoked paprika. Cool at room temperature for at least 20 minutes.

CRAB SALAD

1 tablespoon chopped fresh culantro

2 teaspoons fennel leaves

1 teaspoon finely chopped fresh cilantro

1 teaspoon minced garlic

3 tablespoons canola oil

2 teaspoons lime juice

½ teaspoon chopped serrano pepper

2 teaspoons sliced green onion

Coarse salt and freshly ground black pepper, to taste

1 cup cooked crab meat

REMOULADE

½ cup mayonnaise

1 teaspoon chopped capers

1 teaspoon whole-grain mustard

½ teaspoon minced garlic

½ teaspoon prepared horseradish

1 teaspoon lemon juice

½ teaspoon minced shallots

1 teaspoon chopped fresh parsley

Coarse salt and freshly ground black pepper, to taste

PAPRIKA OIL

½ cup canola oil

1 pinch smoked paprika

FRIED GREEN TOMATOES

2 cups canola oil

1½ cups corn flour

½ cup cornstarch

½ teaspoon ground coriander

1 teaspoon coarse salt

½ teaspoon freshly ground black pepper

⅛ teaspoon ground cayenne

8 (¼-inch-thick) green tomato slices

FRIED GREEN TOMATO-CRAB SALAD

¼ cup canola oil

2 tablespoons capers

1 cup Remoulade, divided

8 Fried Green Tomatoes, divided

1 cup Crab Salad, divided

Paprika Oil, to taste

½ cup shaved fennel, divided

4 fennel fronds, divided

FOR FRIED GREEN TOMATOES

1 With caution, heat canola oil in a Dutch oven over medium heat until it reaches 325°F. Combine corn flour, cornstarch, ground coriander, salt, pepper, and cayenne in a pie plate.

2 Dip both sides of the tomato slices in corn flour mix and shake off excess flour. Carefully fry in oil, turning once, for 2 to 3 minutes on each side, until golden brown.

3 Drain on paper towels. Keep warm until ready to serve.

FOR FRIED GREEN TOMATO-CRAB SALAD

1 Heat canola oil in a small sauté pan for 5 minutes, until hot. Add capers and fry for 2 minutes, until crispy. Drain on paper towels.

2 Spoon ¼ cup Remoulade on the bottom of each plate. Place 1 Fried Green Tomato in the center of each plate and lean a second tomato against the side of the first.

3 Top each with ¼ cup Crab Salad, a drizzle of Paprika Oil, fried capers, shaved fennel, and a fennel frond.

TACOS DE CAMARÓN (TEMPURA SHRIMP)

The surprise is the tangy, magenta-colored hibiscus flower with a cranberry-like sweetness. Find them online or in specialty stores, and use leftover dried hibiscus to make a delicious tart tea. Serve these tacos with a crisp Spanish albariño.

SERVES 4

INTRODUCED 2016 • JARDIN DE FIESTAS OUTDOOR KITCHEN

HIBISCUS FLOWER GARNISH

6 cups water

½ cup dried culinary hibiscus

2 tablespoons canola oil

1 medium white onion, thinly sliced

ROASTED TOMATO SALSA

3 Roma tomatoes, cored

½ white onion, chopped into large pieces

2 tomatillos, husks removed, rinsed

1 garlic clove

1 teaspoon sugar

1 teaspoon coarse salt

½ cup white vinegar

FOR HIBISCUS FLOWER GARNISH

1. Bring water to a boil in a large saucepan; add culinary hibiscus. Steep until flowers are rehydrated and soft, 3 to 6 minutes. Drain and discard water; roughly chop hibiscus and set aside.

2. Heat canola oil in a large skillet; add onions and chopped hibiscus. Sauté until onions are softened, about 3 to 5 minutes. Keep warm until ready to serve.

FOR ROASTED TOMATO SALSA

1. Preheat broiler. Place oven rack in closest position to the broiler. Line a sheet pan with foil.

2. Combine tomatoes, onions, tomatillos, and garlic on prepared sheet pan. Broil 8 minutes, until softened and charred in places. Cool until soft enough to handle.

3. Roughly dice vegetables and place in a medium-sized saucepan over medium heat. Add sugar, salt, and vinegar. Simmer until thickened, about 8 to 10 minutes. Set aside until ready to serve.

FOR TEMPURA SHRIMP

1. Whisk together flour, Tajín, cornstarch and salt in a medium-sized bowl. Slowly add beer, whisking until combined.

2. Add vegetable oil to a heavy-bottom pot to a depth of 2 inches. With caution, heat oil over medium heat to 350°F.

3. Dredge shrimp, one at a time, in batter. Shake off excess and gently lower into oil. Do not overcrowd pot. Carefully fry 3 to 4 minutes, until golden. Transfer cooked shrimp to a plate lined with paper towels.

4. To serve, warm tortillas in a dry skillet. Place 3 shrimp in each tortilla; spoon salsa, then Hibiscus Flower Garnish, over top.

TEMPURA SHRIMP

1¼ cups all-purpose flour

1 tablespoon Tajín seasoning or chili powder

1 tablespoon cornstarch

1 teaspoon fine salt

1½ cups light beer

Vegetable oil, for frying

24 medium shrimp, peeled, deveined

8 medium flour tortillas, for serving

KALE SALAD WITH DRIED CHERRIES, ALMONDS, AND GOAT CHEESE

Lots of fiber, plenty of protein, and dried fruit for a touch of sweetness make this a healthful starter or a main dish. Pair all that goodness with a dry, crisp sauvignon blanc.

SERVES 6-8 AS A SIDE (OR 4 AS AN ENTRÉE)

INTRODUCED 2016 • FLORIDA FRESH OUTDOOR KITCHEN

FOR KALE SALAD

Mix together all ingredients in large bowl.

FOR WHITE BALSAMIC VINAIGRETTE

Place shallots, vinegar, and honey in blender or food processor. Blend on low and slowly add extra-virgin olive oil until blended. Season with salt and pepper.

TO SERVE

Toss salad with desired amount of White Balsamic Vinaigrette. Divide among plates and sprinkle with goat cheese and toasted almonds. Refrigerate any unused vinaigrette.

KALE SALAD

½ bunch kale leaves, tough stems removed, chopped (approximately 2 cups)

6 fresh brussels sprouts, stems removed, sliced thin lengthwise

2 cups broccoli slaw mix

½ cup chopped radicchio leaves

½ cup finely shredded green cabbage

1 cup cooked red quinoa (approximately ⅓ cup uncooked; follow package directions)

½ cup dried cherries

WHITE BALSAMIC VINAIGRETTE

¼ cup minced shallots

½ cup white balsamic vinegar

2 tablespoons honey

1¼ cups extra-virgin olive oil

Coarse salt and freshly ground pepper, to taste

TOPPINGS

½ cup crumbled goat cheese

½ cup toasted sliced almonds

ROASTED CORN SALAD

STARTERS & SMALL PLATES

A perfect side dish for pork ribs (as shown in the photo), grilled fish or roast pork—or delicious all by itself. Roasting the corn in the husk results in the best texture and brings out the sweetness.

SERVES 4-6

INTRODUCED 2016 • THE SMOKEHOUSE: BARBECUE AND BREWS OUTDOOR KITCHEN

FOR ROASTED CORN

1. Heat grill to medium. Pull outer husks down ear to base. Strip silk by hand, then fold husks back into place. Soak ears of corn in cold water with 1 tablespoon salt for 20 minutes.

2. Remove corn from water and shake off excess. Place corn directly on grill, turning every few minutes until kernels are tender when pierced with a knife, about 15 minutes.

3. Remove from grill, remove husks, and cool completely. Cut kernels from cobs.

FOR ROASTED POBLANO

1. Heat a grill or griddle until very hot. Place whole pepper on cooking surface and cook until skin is completely black and flesh is soft, turning often, about 3 to 5 minutes per side.

2. Remove from grill and cover so that pepper will steam for 10 to 15 minutes. Peel blackened skin, remove seeds, and dice.

FOR ROASTED CORN SALAD

1. Combine Roasted Corn, Roasted Poblano, jalapeño peppers, red onions, and red pepper in a medium-sized mixing bowl.

2. In a separate smaller bowl, whisk together mayonnaise and lime juice. Stir in cilantro. Pour over vegetables, stirring well.

3. Season with salt and pepper. Then cover and refrigerate until ready to serve.

ROASTED CORN

8 ears corn, still in husks

1 tablespoon coarse salt

ROASTED POBLANO

1 fresh poblano pepper

ROASTED CORN SALAD

Roasted Corn

Roasted Poblano

2 jalapeño peppers, diced

1 small red onion, diced

1 sweet red pepper, diced

½ cup mayonnaise

1 cup fresh lime juice

¼ cup chopped fresh cilantro

Coarse salt and freshly ground black pepper, to taste

EGGPLANT SCALLOP WITH ROMESCO SAUCE AND ROASTED SPAGHETTI SQUASH

Don't be confused: there are no scallops *or* pasta in this dish. The eggplant is served in overlapping circles, thus the scalloped edge. And the "spaghetti" is a squash that shreds into pieces resembling spaghetti strands.

SERVES 6

INTRODUCED 2014 • URBAN FARM EATS OUTDOOR KITCHEN

FOR ROASTED SPAGHETTI SQUASH

1 Preheat oven to 350°F. Carefully cut squash in half and remove seeds. Place cut side down in a roasting pan; add water until it reaches ¼ inch up sides of pan.

2 Cover pan with foil and roast 30 to 40 minutes until tender. Use a fork to remove flesh in long strands.

3 Place squash strands in a large bowl; toss with extra-virgin olive oil and season with salt and pepper to taste. Set aside and keep warm.

FOR ROMESCO SAUCE

1 Preheat oven to 375°F; line a baking sheet with parchment paper and set aside.

2 Core tomatoes and cut a small X in the bottom of each.

3 Place tomatoes, garlic, bell pepper, poblano pepper, Anaheim chile, and onion in a bowl and toss with 2 tablespoons extra-virgin olive oil, salt, and pepper.

ROASTED SPAGHETTI SQUASH

1 medium spaghetti squash (about 3¼ pounds)

1 tablespoon extra-virgin olive oil

Coarse salt and freshly ground black pepper, to taste

ROMESCO SAUCE

4 Roma tomatoes

4 garlic cloves, peeled

1 small red bell pepper, halved, seeds removed

1 poblano pepper, halved, seeds removed

1 Anaheim chile, halved, seeds removed

1 small onion, peeled and cut into quarters

¼ cup extra-virgin olive oil, divided

½ teaspoon coarse salt

¼ teaspoon freshly ground black pepper

½ cup Marcona almonds

1 tablespoon canned chopped piquillo peppers

4 Place vegetables on prepared baking sheet, and roast 1 hour.

5 Heat remaining oil in a sauté pan over medium-high heat and add almonds. Sauté until golden brown, 2 to 3 minutes.

6 When vegetables are done roasting, carefully peel peppers and tomatoes. Place vegetables, sautéed almonds and oil, piquillo peppers, vinegar, and smoked paprika in a blender. Purée until smooth and thick. Keep warm until ready to serve.

FOR EGGPLANT SCALLOP

1 Slice off stem and root ends of eggplant; cut into 4 (2-inch-thick) slices.

2 Combine salt, pepper, and smoked paprika in a small bowl. Evenly sprinkle spice mixture over eggplant slices.

3 Heat oil in a sauté pan over medium-high heat. Sauté eggplant slices until golden brown and tender, about 3 to 5 minutes per side.

TO SERVE

1 Place a dollop of Romesco Sauce on each serving plate. Then place a serving of Roasted Spaghetti Squash next to sauce.

2 Overlap slices of eggplant between the two so that it is leaning on the squash and also touching the sauce. Drizzle with extra-virgin olive oil and top with micro greens.

2 tablespoons sherry vinegar

1 teaspoon smoked paprika

EGGPLANT SCALLOP

1 Japanese eggplant

1 teaspoon coarse salt

¼ teaspoon freshly ground black pepper

¼ teaspoon smoked paprika

2 tablespoons extra-virgin olive oil, plus more for serving

Micro greens, for serving

SHRIMP AND STONE-GROUND GRITS WITH ANDOUILLE SAUSAGE AND SWEET CORN

MAINS & SIDES

Brunch or supper, this classic Southern combo of spicy pork sausage and fresh shrimp over creamy grits is a crowd pleaser. If you can't find andouille, you can substitute chorizo or any smoked sausage.

SERVES 4

INTRODUCED 2016 • FLORIDA FRESH OUTDOOR KITCHEN

FOR BROTH

1   Heat olive oil in a large saucepan over medium-high heat; add andouille, cooking until golden brown, about 5 minutes. Add onions, and garlic, cooking until translucent. Add celery, peppers, and Cajun seasoning, cooking until tender, about 5 to 6 minutes more.

2   Add broth; bring to a boil, then reduce heat to medium-low and simmer 30 minutes.

3   Purée with a hand blender, or carefully pour broth into a blender and blend until completely puréed. Blend in butter with hand blender or add butter to blender, and blend again until well combined. Then stir in tomato and cilantro.

FOR GRITS

Bring water to a boil; whisk in grits and salt. Cook, whisking, 1 minute. Cook 5 minutes, stirring occasionally, or until grits are tender. Stir in butter and Parmesan.

BROTH

1 teaspoon olive oil

¼ cup diced andouille sausage

½ cup finely diced yellow onion

1 tablespoon minced garlic

½ cup finely diced celery

½ cup finely diced green peppers

1 teaspoon Cajun seasoning

4 cups chicken broth

½ cup unsalted butter

½ cup finely diced tomato

1 tablespoon finely chopped fresh cilantro

GRITS

4 cups water

1 cup quick grits

1 teaspoon coarse salt

½ cup unsalted butter, room temperature, cut into pieces

½ cup grated Parmesan cheese

FOR SHRIMP

1 Carefully heat olive oil in a large skillet over medium-high heat. Add andouille, cooking until golden brown, about 5 minutes.

2 Add onions, pepper, celery, and Cajun seasoning, cooking until vegetables soften, about 4 minutes.

3 Add shrimp and cook until opaque and cooked through, 2 to 4 minutes. Stir in corn, cooking 1 minute more.

TO SERVE

Divide grits among 4 serving bowls. Divide shrimp and vegetable mixture among grits. Then ladle on broth, and top with cilantro.

SHRIMP

1 teaspoon olive oil

¾ cup finely diced andouille sausage

½ cup finely diced yellow onion

½ cup finely diced green pepper

½ cup finely diced celery

½ teaspoon Cajun seasoning

16–20 medium fresh shrimp, peeled and deveined (about 1 pound)

½ cup fresh corn

Finely chopped fresh cilantro, for serving

JERK-SPICED GROUPER WITH MANGO SALSA AND CHAYOTE AND GREEN PAPAYA SLAW

MAINS & SIDES

The heat of Jamaican-inspired jerk spice, sweet mango salsa, and a crunchy green papaya slaw create a trifecta of deliciousness. Use a julienne peeler for super-thin strips of chayote and papaya. You can substitute chicken for grouper if you prefer. Serve with an ice-cold Caribbean beer.

SERVES 4

INTRODUCED 2016 • LA ISLA FRESCA OUTDOOR KITCHEN

FOR CHAYOTE AND GREEN PAPAYA SLAW

1. Combine rice vinegar, lime juice, oil, and cilantro in a food processor; mix until well combined.

2. Combine chayote, green papaya, onions, salt, and pepper in a large bowl; toss to combine. Add vinaigrette, tossing to coat vegetables. Refrigerate until ready to serve (for up to 3 days).

FOR MANGO SALSA

1. Combine all ingredients in a medium-sized saucepan over medium-high heat. Bring to a simmer, stirring constantly, until sugar is dissolved.

2. Lower heat to medium-low; simmer 25 minutes, stirring frequently, until mixture is thickened. Set aside.

CHAYOTE AND GREEN PAPAYA SLAW

¼ cup rice vinegar

2 tablespoons fresh lime juice

2 tablespoons olive oil

1 tablespoon finely chopped fresh cilantro

2 cups julienned chayote squash

2 cups julienned green papaya

½ cup julienned red onion

¼ teaspoon coarse salt

⅛ teaspoon freshly ground black pepper

MANGO SALSA

2½ cups diced fresh or frozen (thawed) mango

1 (1-inch) piece peeled fresh ginger

1 Scotch bonnet pepper, minced

1 garlic clove, minced

½ cup cider vinegar

½ cup firmly packed light brown sugar

½ cup raisins

¼ teaspoon coarse salt

Freshly ground black pepper, to taste

JERK-SPICED GROUPER

3 garlic cloves, chopped

1 medium onion, chopped

2 scotch bonnet peppers, chopped

1 cup chopped green onion

½ cup soy sauce

1 tablespoon brown sugar

2 teaspoons ground allspice

2 teaspoons chopped fresh thyme

1 teaspoon ground nutmeg

1 teaspoon ground cinnamon

½ teaspoon ground black pepper

½ cup plus 1 tablespoon olive oil, divided

4 (6-ounce) grouper filets *or* 4 (6-ounce) boneless, skinless chicken breasts

FOR JERK-SPICED GROUPER

1 Combine garlic, onions, scotch bonnet pepper, green onions, soy sauce, brown sugar, allspice, thyme, nutmeg, cinnamon, and black pepper in a food processor; pulse to combine. Add ½ cup olive oil and process until puréed.

2 Place marinade in a medium-sized bowl. Add grouper or chicken and completely cover with marinade. Refrigerate 4 to 6 hours.

3 Heat remaining 1 tablespoon olive oil in a large skillet over medium-high heat. Place grouper in pan and sear 3 minutes. Flip and cook until just cooked through, 3 to 5 minutes, depending on thickness of fillets. *If you prefer the chicken, preheat oven to 350°F. Heat remaining 1 tablespoon olive oil in an ovenproof sauté pan over medium-high heat. Shake excess marinade off chicken breasts and place in sauté pan. Cook 3 minutes, then flip and place pan in preheated oven. Cook 15 to 20 minutes, until cooked through.*

4 Serve with slaw and chutney.

BONELESS IMPOSSIBLE™ KOREAN SHORT RIBS WITH CILANTRO-LIME RICE, DANMUJI SLAW, AND KIMCHEE MAYONNAISE

This recipe takes some time, but the authentic flavors of Korean barbecue sauce and the seasoning create a savory, spicy "rib."

SERVES 6

INTRODUCED 2021 • TROWEL & TRELLIS OUTDOOR KITCHEN, HOSTED BY IMPOSSIBLE FOODS

FOR BONELESS IMPOSSIBLE™ SHORT RIBS

1. Preheat oven to 250°F. Line 9 × 5-inch loaf pan with parchment paper and set aside.

2. Combine Impossible™ Beef, five spice powder, gochujang paste, garlic, chickpea flour, and salt in large bowl and stir until fully combined. Spoon into prepared loaf pan and pack tightly, making sure the top is smooth.

3. Cover loaf pan tightly with foil. Fill 9 × 13-inch pan halfway with water. Set loaf pan inside of water bath.

4. Bake for 1 hour, until Impossible™ Beef reaches an internal temperature of 145°F. Remove loaf pan from water bath and cool at room temperature for 30 minutes. Once pan is cool enough to handle, remove loaf from pan. Wrap in plastic wrap and refrigerate for 24 hours.

5. Remove from plastic wrap and slice into eighteen ½-inch-thick rectangles.

BONELESS IMPOSSIBLE™ SHORT RIBS

1 pound Impossible™ Beef Made From Plants

¼ teaspoon Chinese five spice powder

1 tablespoon gochujang paste

1 clove garlic, minced

2 tablespoons chickpea flour

1 teaspoon salt

KOREAN BARBECUE SAUCE

1 cup soy sauce

2 tablespoons sesame oil

2 tablespoons mirin

2 tablespoons rice wine vinegar

2 tablespoons ginger paste

1½ teaspoons minced garlic

1½ teaspoons sambal oelek chili paste

⅓ cup brown sugar

2 cups, plus 2 tablespoons, water, divided

2 tablespoons cornstarch

FOR KOREAN BARBECUE SAUCE

1. Combine soy sauce, sesame oil, mirin, rice wine vinegar, ginger paste, garlic, sambal oelek, brown sugar, and 2 cups water in a medium-sized saucepan. Bring to simmer over medium-low heat. Continue simmering for 30 minutes.

2. Combine 2 tablespoons water with cornstarch in a small bowl. Slowly whisk into sauce and simmer until barbecue sauce is thick and sticky. Keep warm until ready to serve.

FOR DANMUJI SLAW

1. Combine water, rice wine vinegar, garlic cloves, bay leaf, peppercorns, turmeric, coarse salt, and sugar in a medium-sized saucepan. Bring to boil over high heat.

2. Remove brine from heat and let rest for 30 minutes.

3. Place daikon and carrots in a medium-sized glass bowl. Pour cooled brine over vegetables. Rest for 30 minutes before serving.

DANMUJI SLAW

1 cup water

1 cup rice wine vinegar

2 cloves garlic, halved

1 bay leaf

¼ teaspoon black peppercorns

½ teaspoon ground turmeric

1½ teaspoons coarse salt

1½ teaspoons sugar

½ pound daikon radish, julienned

3 medium carrots, peeled and julienned

(RECIPE CONTINUES ON PAGE 104)

BONELESS IMPOSSIBLE™ KOREAN SHORT RIBS WITH CILANTRO-LIME RICE, DANMUJI SLAW, AND KIMCHEE MAYONNAISE

(CONTINUED)

FOR CILANTRO-LIME RICE

1. Place rice and water in a medium-sized saucepan. Bring to rolling boil, uncovered, on medium-high heat. Then reduce heat to simmer, cover with lid, and cook for 12 minutes, until water is absorbed by rice.

2. Remove from heat and let rice stand for 10 minutes. Fluff with spatula or rice paddle. Then add lime juice, zest, and cilantro. Season with salt, to taste, and keep warm until ready to serve.

FOR KIMCHEE MAYONNAISE

Combine kimchee base and plant-based mayonnaise in a small bowl. Refrigerate until ready to serve.

TO SERVE

1. Bring a large stockpot of water to boil. Season generously with salt and add bok choy. Cook for 2 minutes, until tender. Place in ice bath with slotted spoon. Set aside.

2. Heat oil in large sauté pan over medium heat for 5 minutes, until hot. Add sliced short ribs and cook for 1 to 2 minutes per side, until crispy. Add barbecue sauce to fully coat ribs.

3. Place 1 cup Cilantro-Lime Rice in each bowl. Top with 3 slices of short rib and glaze with additional barbecue sauce, if desired. Add large spoonful of slaw to each bowl. Place ½ head of baby bok choy in each bowl. Drizzle with mayonnaise and top with black sesame seeds.

CILANTRO-LIME RICE

2 cups jasmine rice

2½ cups water

1 tablespoon lime juice

Zest of 1 lime

1 tablespoon finely chopped cilantro

Coarse salt, to taste

KIMCHEE MAYONNAISE

1 tablespoon kimchee base

½ cup plant-based mayonnaise

TOPPINGS

3 baby bok choy, cut in half

2 tablespoons olive oil

1 tablespoon black sesame seeds

URBAN MARY

Feel free to play with all the ingredients to suit your style in this refreshing Bloody Mary!

SERVES 1

INTRODUCED 2016 • URBAN FARM EATS OUTDOOR KITCHEN

Stir together Bloody Mary mix, lime juice, Worcestershire sauce, vodka, salt, and pepper in a tall glass. Fill glass with ice, then pour mixture into a second glass. Pour back and forth a couple of times to mix well. Top with pickled green bean and add hot sauce, to taste.

4½ ounces favorite Bloody Mary mix

2 teaspoons fresh lime juice

2 teaspoons Worcestershire sauce

½ ounce vodka

Coarse salt and freshly ground black pepper, to taste

1 cup ice

Favorite pickled green bean, for serving

Favorite hot sauce, to taste

HUGO COCKTAIL

Said to have been invented in a small Alpine town in Italy just south of the Austrian border, this refreshing summer spritzer is popular all across Europe.

5 ounces sparkling wine or prosecco

1 teaspoon elderflower syrup

1 sprig mint

SERVES 1

INTRODUCED 2016 • BAUERNMARKT FARMER'S MARKET OUTDOOR KITCHEN

Pour sparkling wine in a champagne flute. Add syrup, and top with a mint sprig.

FRUSHI

The textures and flavors of pineapple, strawberries, and cantaloupe are a great combination, but you could use almost any seasonal fruit in this fun version of a sushi roll. You can find soy wrappers online or in many grocery stores.

MAKES 16 ROLLS

INTRODUCED 2016 • HANAMI OUTDOOR KITCHEN

2 cups cooked sushi rice, prepared according to package directions

1 tablespoon cream of coconut

16 soy wrappers

16 fresh strawberries, hulled and quartered

½ cantaloupe, cut into 4-inch-long by ¼-inch-wide rectangles

½ pineapple, peeled and cored, cut into 4-inch-long by ¼-inch-wide rectangles

Toasted coconut, for topping

Whipped cream, for serving

Strawberry syrup, for serving

1. Let sushi rice cool slightly. Stir in cream of coconut. Set aside to cool to room temperature.

2. Lay one soy wrapper on flat surface. Place about ¼ cup sushi rice on soy wrapper, pressing with moistened fingers to cover whole sheet.

3. Place one piece each of pineapple and cantaloupe and four pieces of strawberry in center of rice-covered sheet.

4. Starting at one end, fold about one third of roll up, then roll sheet into cylinder, keeping fruit in the middle. Moisten soy wrapper to seal.

5. Cut into 4 equal pieces. Repeat with remaining ingredients. Top with toasted coconut, and serve with whipped cream drizzled with strawberry syrup on the side.

CITRUS-BAKED BRIE

SWEET ENDINGS & DESSERTS

Lemon marmalade and cold fresh blueberries cut the richness of the warm Brie in this sweet-salty treat. And while the Marcona almonds might seem like an afterthought, they are addictively delicious.

SERVES 8

INTRODUCED 2023 • THE CITRUS BLOSSOM OUTDOOR KITCHEN

FOR LIMONCELLO BLUEBERRIES

Wash and dry blueberries. Combine blueberries, sugar, limoncello, lemon zest, and thyme in a small bowl. Refrigerate at least 4 hours, or for up to one day.

FOR LEMON MARMALADE FILLING

Combine lemon pie filling and orange marmalade in a small bowl. Refrigerate until ready to use.

FOR SPICED MARCONA ALMONDS

1. Preheat oven to 350°F. Line a baking sheet with parchment paper or a silicone baking mat. Set aside.

2. Combine sugar and water in medium-sized bowl. Stir until dissolved. Then add almonds to mixture and stir until well coated. Season with cayenne pepper and salt and pour onto baking sheet.

3. Bake for 10 to 12 minutes, stirring once, until browned. Set aside until ready to use.

FOR CITRUS-BAKED BRIE

1. Preheat oven to 400°F. Cut thawed puff pastry sheets into 4 × 4-inch squares. Cut Brie cheese into 8 equal pieces.

2. Place 1 tablespoon lemon marmalade in the center of each square. Top with one piece of Brie cheese.

LIMONCELLO BLUEBERRIES

1 cup blueberries

⅓ cup sugar

2 tablespoons limoncello

1 teaspoon lemon zest

1 teaspoon finely chopped thyme

LEMON MARMALADE FILLING

3 tablespoons lemon pie filling

⅓ cup orange marmalade

SPICED MARCONA ALMONDS

½ cup Marcona almonds

2 tablespoons sugar

2 tablespoons water

½ teaspoon cayenne pepper

½ teaspoon salt

CITRUS-BAKED BRIE

2 sheets puff pastry, thawed

8-ounce wheel of Brie cheese

Lemon Marmalade Filling

1 egg yolk

2 tablespoons water

3 To fold the puff pastry, bring the diagonal ends together so that all 4 sides meet, then twist, making sure to seal any open ends.

4 Combine egg yolk and water in small bowl. Brush on puff pastry.

5 Bake for 12 to 14 minutes until Brie cheese is melted and puff pastry is golden brown.

6 Remove from oven and top with Limoncello Blueberries and Spiced Marcona Almonds. Serve warm.

HONEY-MASCARPONE CHEESECAKE

This is so much more than a cheesecake, starting with the chiffon cake that sits atop, and a scoop of ice cream for good measure. Finish the dish with pure local honey if you can find it.

SERVES 12

INTRODUCED 2018 · HONEY BEE-STRO OUTDOOR KITCHEN

FOR VANILLA CHIFFON CAKE

1. Preheat oven to 300°F. Line a baking sheet with parchment paper.

2. Sift cake flour, baking powder, salt, and 1 cup sugar into bowl of an electric mixer. Add eggs, vegetable oil, and milk. Beat on medium speed for 2 minutes, until mixed.

3. Whip egg whites and remaining ½ cup sugar in a clean mixing bowl with electric mixer on high speed until medium peaks form. Gently fold egg whites into batter.

4. Spread into prepared pan and bake for 20 to 25 minutes, until golden brown. Cool cake for at least 20 minutes.

FOR HONEY-MASCARPONE CHEESECAKE

1. Preheat oven to 350°F. Tightly wrap the outside of a 9-inch springform pan in heavy aluminum foil.

2. Beat cream cheese, mascarpone cheese, and sugar in the bowl of an electric mixer fitted with a paddle attachment until smooth. Add lemon juice and vanilla extract. Add eggs one at a time, on medium speed, beating until just blended.

VANILLA CHIFFON CAKE

2 cups cake flour

1½ teaspoons baking powder

1 teaspoon salt

1½ cups sugar, divided

3 eggs

½ cup vegetable oil

½ cup whole milk

8 egg whites

HONEY-MASCARPONE CHEESECAKE

2 (8-ounce) packages cream cheese, room temperature

2 (8-ounce) containers mascarpone cheese, room temperature

1¼ cups sugar

2 teaspoons lemon juice

1 teaspoon vanilla extract

4 eggs

3 Pour cheesecake mixture into prepared pan. Place springform pan into a roasting pan and fill the roasting pan with water, until it comes halfway up the sides of the springform pan.

4 Bake for 1 hour and 5 minutes, until the center of the cheesecake moves slightly when shaken. Cut a 9-inch circle from the Vanilla Chiffon Cake and place directly on top of the cheesecake.

5 Cool for one hour at room temperature. Refrigerate, covered, for at least 8 hours. Remove from pan right before serving.

TO SERVE

Place cheesecake on a plate and drizzle with honey. Serve with a scoop of ice cream.

TOPPINGS

Honey

Vanilla (or honey) ice cream

CHOCOLATE CAKE WITH WHISKEY CARAMEL AND MAPLE CUSTARD SAUCE

New at the 2023 festival, this rich cake, similar to a brownie, calls for a lot of butter—but it works. A dip in warm simple syrup, a drizzle of caramel sauce on the plate, then custard in the center—it's an extravaganza. Make the custard a day or two ahead so you can focus on the caramel sauce as the cakes are baking.

SERVES 12

INTRODUCED 2023 • NORTHERN BLOOM OUTDOOR KITCHEN

MAPLE CUSTARD SAUCE

½ cup whole milk

½ cup whipping cream

4 large egg yolks

2 tablespoons sugar

3 tablespoons maple syrup

2 teaspoons maple extract, optional

FOR MAPLE CUSTARD SAUCE

1 Combine milk and whipping cream in medium-sized saucepan. Bring to a simmer over medium heat.

2 Whisk egg yolks, sugar, and maple syrup in a medium-sized bowl until egg yolks are pale. Slowly whisk half of the warm cream mix into the egg yolks. Return to saucepan. Cook over low heat, stirring constantly for 5 minutes, or until custard coats the back of a spoon.

3 Stir in maple extract, if using. Strain custard into a medium-sized bowl. Cover and refrigerate for up to 2 days.

OPPOSITE, BOTTOM: Floating flower beds are a signature of the annual EPCOT International Flower & Garden Festival, as shown here from 2021 in the waters near the IMAGINATION! pavilion.

(RECIPE CONTINUES ON PAGE 114)

EPCOT INTERNATIONAL FLOWER & GARDEN FESTIVAL · WALT DISNEY WORLD

CHOCOLATE CAKE WITH WHISKEY CARAMEL AND MAPLE CUSTARD SAUCE

FOR WHISKEY SIMPLE SYRUP

Combine water and sugar in a small saucepan. Bring to a boil. Remove from heat and stir in whiskey. Keep warm until ready to use.

FOR CHOCOLATE CAKE

1. Preheat oven to 350°F. Grease twelve mini fluted tube pans (each 3½- to 4-inch round), and set aside. Sift flour, cocoa powder, and salt into a medium-sized bowl, and set aside.

2. Beat eggs and sugar in the bowl of an electric mixer fitted with a paddle attachment on medium speed for 3 minutes, until eggs are pale in color. Add vanilla and mix until combined.

3. Add ½ cup butter and a third of the flour mixture. Then mix on low speed until combined. Repeat with remaining butter and flour mixture.

4. Add melted chocolate and stir until combined. Batter can be used immediately or refrigerated for up to one day.

5. Spoon batter into a pastry bag with a large round tip. Pipe batter into each fluted tube pan, filling until two-thirds full.

6. Bake for 25 to 30 minutes, when tops are shiny and set, with a consistency similar to a brownie. Cool completely before removing from molds.

WHISKEY SIMPLE SYRUP

¾ cup water

1 cup sugar

¼ cup whiskey

CHOCOLATE CAKE

¾ cup all-purpose flour

1 cup unsweetened cocoa powder

1 teaspoon salt

3 large eggs

½ cup sugar plus 3 tablespoons, divided

1½ cups unsalted butter, room temperature, divided

6 ounces semisweet chocolate, melted

FOR WHISKEY CARAMEL SAUCE

1. Combine sugar and water in a medium-sized saucepan. Cook over medium heat, swirling the pan and brushing down the sides with a pastry brush as needed, until sugar dissolves.

2. Continue cooking undisturbed, for 5 to 7 minutes, until medium-amber caramel forms. Then carefully add cream and simmer, whisking constantly for 1 to 2 minutes, until caramel is smooth.

3. Cool for 5 minutes, then stir in whiskey and sea salt. Set aside until ready to serve.

TO SERVE

Unmold the chocolate cakes and place on a wire rack above a baking sheet. Dip each cake 1 to 2 times in warm Whiskey Simple Syrup, letting excess syrup drip onto baking sheet. Spread 1 to 2 tablespoons of Whiskey Caramel Sauce around each plate, and then place cake in the center. Fill center of each cake with Maple Custard Sauce.

WHISKEY CARAMEL SAUCE

⅔ cup sugar

2 tablespoons water

½ cup heavy cream, room temperature

1 tablespoon whiskey

⅛ teaspoon sea salt

ABOVE: For the 2021 Taste of EPCOT International Flower & Garden Festival, a patchwork of Mickey Mouse flower beds lined the shore in front of the IMAGINATION! pavilion.

BUTTERMILK CAKE WITH BERRY COMPOTE (GLUTEN FRIENDLY)

Buttermilk is a tenderizer and adds loft and a lighter texture, and the tart berries soak into the cake, made with gluten-free flour. You can use all-purpose flour instead of gluten-free.

MAKES 1 (8-INCH) CAKE

INTRODUCED 2019 • ARBOR AT GARDENERS TERRACE

GLUTEN-FRIENDLY STREUSEL

¼ cup unsalted butter, softened

¼ cup brown sugar

½ teaspoon vanilla extract

1 teaspoon ground cinnamon

¾ cup gluten-free one-to-one flour

GLUTEN-FRIENDLY BUTTERMILK CAKE

1¼ cups gluten-free one-to-one flour

¼ teaspoon salt

½ teaspoon baking powder

½ cup buttermilk

1 teaspoon vanilla extract

½ cup vegetable oil

2 eggs

¾ cup sugar

FOR GLUTEN-FRIENDLY STREUSEL

Cream together butter, brown sugar, vanilla extract, and cinnamon in a medium-sized bowl until smooth and creamy. Add gluten-free flour, and stir by hand with a spatula or large fork, mixing until pea-sized crumbs are formed. Then set aside.

FOR GLUTEN-FRIENDLY BUTTERMILK CAKE

1   Preheat oven to 325°F. Sift together gluten-free flour, salt, and baking powder in a small bowl. Set aside. Then blend buttermilk, vanilla extract, and vegetable oil in a 2-cup measuring cup. Set aside.

2   Whip eggs and sugar in a large bowl, using an electric hand mixer on a high speed, until light and airy, approximately 2 minutes, scraping sides halfway through.

3   Alternate adding flour mixture and buttermilk mixture into the whipped eggs in two stages on low speed, scraping sides halfway through and at end.

4   Pour batter into a greased 8-inch cake pan. Sprinkle streusel evenly on top. Bake for 30 to 32 minutes or until inserted toothpick comes out clean. Allow to cool.

FOR BERRY COMPOTE

Wash berries, and drain but do not dry. Then place in a microwave-safe bowl. Add sugar and lemon juice, cover, and microwave 3 minutes on high. Stir to dissolve sugar, and allow to cool.

TO SERVE

Serve sliced cake with 1 to 2 tablespoons Berry Compote, drizzled over cake. Add 1 scoop ice cream or a dollop of whipped cream on the side.

BERRY COMPOTE

3 total cups seasonal berries (red raspberries, quartered strawberries, blueberries, blackberries)

3 tablespoons sugar (add more or less for desired sweetness)

Juice of ½ lemon

TOPPINGS

Gluten-friendly vanilla ice cream

Whipped cream

PLANT-BASED TRES LECHES CAKE

Just the right amount of sweet in this plant-based sweet made with vanilla cake soaked in oat, almond and coconut milks with a finish of toasted coconut.

SERVES 9

INTRODUCED 2022 • LA ISLA FRESCA OUTDOOR KITCHEN

PLANT-BASED TRES LECHES CAKE

- 1½ cups cake flour
- 1 teaspoon baking powder
- ⅛ teaspoon salt
- ⅓ cup canola oil
- 1¼ cups sugar, divided
- 1 teaspoon vanilla extract
- 1 teaspoon lemon extract
- 1 teaspoon lemon zest
- 1¼ cups plant-based egg substitute
- 1 cup oat milk
- ½ cup almond milk
- ½ cup cream of coconut

FOR PLANT-BASED TRES LECHES CAKE

1. Preheat oven to 325°F. Lightly grease a 9 × 9-inch cake pan with nonstick cooking spray.

2. Whisk flour, baking powder, and salt in a small mixing bowl; set aside.

3. Combine canola oil, 1 cup sugar, vanilla extract, lemon extract, and lemon zest in the bowl of an electric mixer fitted with a paddle attachment. Mix on low speed for 2 minutes. Increase speed to medium and slowly add egg substitute. Once egg substitute is fully incorporated, reduce speed to low, add half of the flour mixture, and beat until mixed. Add remaining flour on low speed until batter is smooth.

4. Pour batter into prepared pan and bake for 25 to 28 minutes, until toothpick inserted in the center comes out clean. Cool to room temperature.

5. Whisk together oat milk, almond milk, and cream of coconut. If desired, add remaining ¼ cup sugar.

6. Pierce cooled cake with a fork 30 to 40 times. Pour milk mixture over cake. Cover and refrigerate at least one hour.

FOR TOPPINGS

1 Place nondairy whipping cream in the bowl of an electric mixer fitted with a whisk attachment. Whip on high speed until medium peaks form. Refrigerate until ready to serve.

2 Heat a small skillet over medium-low heat for 5 minutes. Add coconut and cook, stirring frequently, for 3 to 5 minutes, until coconut is light brown. Set aside until ready to serve.

TO SERVE

Cut cake into 9 slices. Top each slice with whipped cream and toasted coconut.

TOPPINGS

1½ cups nondairy whipping cream

1 cup shredded coconut

MAPLE PECAN STREUSEL CAKE WITH PRALINE SAUCE

Breakfast, brunch, or dessert, this not-too-sweet cake celebrates the South's buttery pecan. A drizzle of maple syrup and whipped cream fancy it up.

SERVES 12

INTRODUCED 2021 • MAGNOLIA TERRACE OUTDOOR KITCHEN

FOR STREUSEL TOPPING

1 Cream butter, brown sugar, vanilla extract, and cinnamon in the bowl of an electric mixer fitted with a paddle attachment until fluffy.

2 Add flour and stir with a spatula until crumbs form. Set aside until ready to use.

FOR MAPLE PECAN CAKE

1 Preheat oven to 325°F. Grease a fluted tube pan (9-inch round). Sift flour, baking powder, and salt into a medium-sized bowl. Set aside.

2 Combine milk, vegetable oil, and maple extract in a medium-sized bowl, and set aside. Then beat brown sugar and eggs the bowl of an electric mixer fitted with a paddle attachment until eggs are pale in color.

3 Add half of the flour mixture and half of the milk mixture to the brown sugar mixture and combine on low speed. Add remaining flour and milk until combined. Fold in pecans.

4 Pour into prepared pan and top with Streusel Topping. Then bake for 30 to 35 minutes, until a toothpick inserted in the center comes out clean. Cool completely before removing from pan.

STREUSEL TOPPING

¼ cup unsalted butter

¼ cup brown sugar

½ teaspoon vanilla extract

1 teaspoon ground cinnamon

¾ cup all-purpose flour

MAPLE PECAN CAKE

1 cup all-purpose flour

¾ teaspoon baking powder

¼ teaspoon salt

½ cup milk

⅔ cup vegetable oil

2 tablespoons maple extract

1 cup brown sugar

2 eggs

1 cup finely chopped pecans

Streusel Topping

FOR PRALINE SAUCE

1 Preheat oven to 350°F. Line a baking sheet with parchment paper.

2 Place pecans on baking sheet and toast for 4 minutes. Stir, and toast an additional 4 minutes, until browned and fragrant. Set aside.

3 Combine brown sugar, evaporated milk, butter, and corn syrup in a small saucepan. Bring to simmer over medium-low heat and simmer for 3 minutes, stirring constantly, until thick. Stir in toasted pecans, vanilla extract, and salt. Cool slightly before serving.

TO SERVE

Slice cake and top with Praline Sauce.

PRALINE SAUCE

1 cup pecan halves

1¼ cups light brown sugar

¾ cup evaporated milk

2 tablespoons unsalted butter

1 tablespoon corn syrup

1 teaspoon vanilla extract

½ teaspoon salt

PIGGYLICIOUS BACON CUPCAKE

Bacon fat replaces vegetable oil in these sweet-savory cupcakes topped with maple cream cheese and decorated with salty pretzels. Don't count the calories, but for bacon fans, the splurge is worth it.

MAKES 24

INTRODUCED 2014 • THE SMOKEHOUSE: BARBECUE AND BREWS OUTDOOR KITCHEN

FOR BACON CAKE

Follow directions for cake, replacing oil with bacon fat. Fold in bacon. Bake according to instructions.

FOR MAPLE CREAM CHEESE ICING

Cream together cream cheese and butter until light and fluffy in a mixing bowl with a paddle attachment. Then mix in maple syrup. Gradually add powdered sugar until combined.

TO SERVE

Frost cupcakes and top with crushed pretzel twists.

BACON CAKE

Favorite yellow cake mix

Equal amount of bacon fat to replace oil in mix

12 slices bacon, cooked crisp and chopped fine

MAPLE CREAM CHEESE ICING

1 (8-ounce) package cream cheese

¼ cup unsalted butter, softened

1 tablespoon real maple syrup, plus more to taste

2 cups powdered sugar

TOPPING

Crushed pretzel twists

OPPOSITE, BOTTOM: Gardening-themed Donald Duck and Daisy Duck topiaries greeted guests to World Showcase during the 2021 Taste of EPCOT International Flower & Garden Festival.

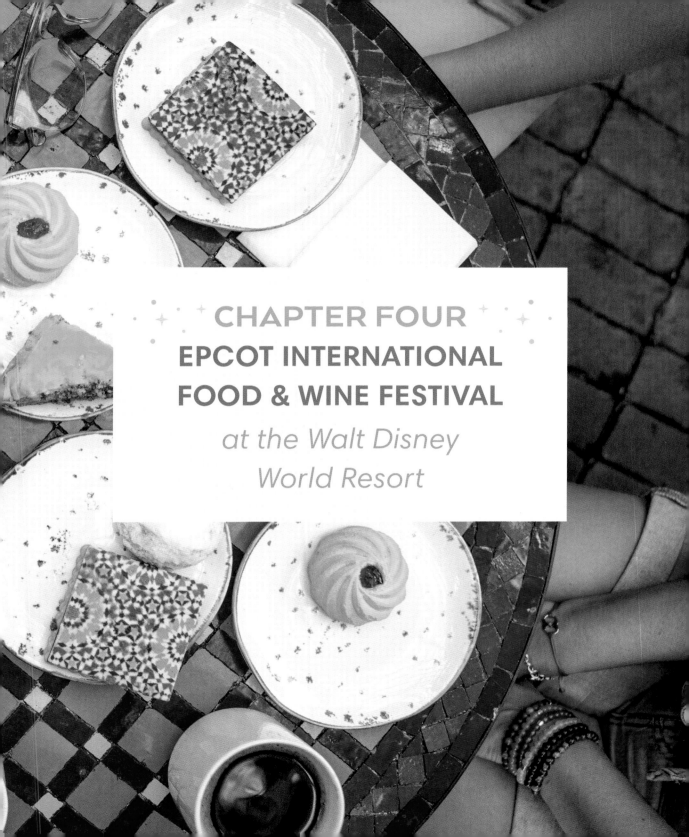

CHAPTER FOUR
EPCOT INTERNATIONAL FOOD & WINE FESTIVAL
at the Walt Disney World Resort

S INCE ITS DEBUT in 1996, the EPCOT International Food & Wine Festival has grown from a thirty-day festival with twenty-five festival marketplaces around World Showcase to more than one hundred days of feasting fun with global marketplaces stretching into World Discovery. Live entertainment, kid-friendly fun, chef demonstrations, and wine seminars make it the most popular festival at Walt Disney World Resort.

THESE PAGES: A scrumptious spread on a Morocco pavilion table in World Showcase at EPCOT (previous pages, 2022). Walt Disney World Resort chefs prepare dessert trays for the France pavilion in World Showcase at EPCOT (above, 2015). For the 2014 EPCOT International Food & Wine Festival, a colorful Chef Mickey topiary scene greets guests (opposite).

BO SSAM (LETTUCE WRAPS WITH ROAST PORK)

A wrap of tender Bibb lettuce is perfect for this slow-roasted pork topped with crunchy kimchee slaw and sesame mayo. (*Bossam* means "wrapped" or "packaged" in Korean.) Serve with Bokbunjajoo, a traditional sweet and delicious Korean fruit wine made from black raspberries.

SERVES 4

INTRODUCED 2015 • SOUTH KOREA GLOBAL MARKETPLACE

ROAST PORK

¼ cup light brown sugar

2 tablespoons coarse salt

2½ pounds boneless pork butt

KIMCHEE SLAW

3 cups napa cabbage

½ cup thinly sliced red onion

½ cup shredded carrot

1 teaspoon minced ginger

1 tablespoon sambal oelek chili paste

1 teaspoon minced garlic

2 tablespoons lime juice

1 tablespoon rice vinegar

1 teaspoon fish sauce

1 tablespoon sugar

FOR ROAST PORK

1 Combine brown sugar and salt in a small bowl. Rub mixture on pork. Place pork in a zip-top bag, and refrigerate for 6 hours or overnight.

2 Preheat oven to 300°F. Remove pork from bag and rinse off sugar and salt; pat dry and place in a small roasting pan.

3 Roast pork for 4½ hours, or until very tender. Shred into bite-size pieces with a fork.

FOR KIMCHEE SLAW

Combine cabbage, onions, and carrot in a large bowl, and set aside. Combine remaining ingredients in a small bowl, and whisk together. Pour dressing over vegetables, and toss to coat. Then cover and refrigerate for 2 hours, or until slaw is wilted.

FOR SESAME MAYONNAISE

1. Toast sesame seeds in a small, dry skillet over medium-high heat, stirring constantly, until light brown and aromatic. Cool.

2. Combine sesame seeds and remaining ingredients in a medium-sized bowl. Whisk to combine, and then refrigerate until ready to use.

FOR BO SSAM

Place 2 to 3 lettuce wraps on each serving plate. Evenly divide Roast Pork among lettuce leaves. Top with Kimchee Slaw and Sesame Mayonnaise. Fold lettuce around fillings.

SESAME MAYONNAISE

1 tablespoon sesame seeds

1 tablespoon water

½ cup mayonnaise

1½ teaspoons toasted sesame oil

1½ teaspoons lemon juice

1 teaspoon granulated garlic

½ teaspoon coarse salt

¼ teaspoon freshly ground black pepper

BO SSAM

6–12 Bibb lettuce leaves

Roast Pork

Kimchee Slaw, to taste

Sesame Mayonnaise, to taste

PORK POT STICKERS

Steamed, then pan-fried to create a crisp bottom crust, Chinese pot stickers are easy to make at home with store-bought wrappers. They freeze well, too, and you can cook them right out of the freezer without defrosting.

SERVES 8

INTRODUCED 2015 • CHINA GLOBAL MARKETPLACE

PORK POT STICKERS

¼ pound napa cabbage

½ pound ground pork

1 tablespoon finely chopped scallion

1 teaspoon finely chopped fresh ginger

¼ teaspoon coarse salt

½ teaspoon sugar

1 tablespoon light soy sauce

½ tablespoon rice vinegar

½ tablespoon sesame oil

32 gyoza (pot sticker) wrappers

½ cup canola oil, divided

⅔ cup hot water

FOR PORK POT STICKERS

1. Separate cabbage leaves from core. Discard core and blanch leaves in a large pot of boiling water for 2 to 3 minutes, or until soft. Remove leaves from pot, and plunge into a bowl of ice water to stop cooking. Drain and pat dry with paper towels. When dry, finely chop.

2. Combine the chopped cabbage, ground pork, scallion, ginger, salt, sugar, soy sauce, rice vinegar, and sesame oil in a large bowl.

3. Working in batches of 3, place about ½ tablespoon of the filling in the center of each wrapper, keeping remaining wrappers covered with a damp cloth.

4. Lightly moisten halfway around edges with a finger dipped in water. Fold each dumpling in half, and firmly pinch the edges to seal.

5. Place the dumplings on a tray lightly dusted with flour, and cover with another damp cloth while you make remaining dumplings.

6. Heat 2 tablespoons of canola oil in a large sauté pan over medium heat, tilting the pan to coat evenly. Arrange 8 to 10 dumplings in the pan in one layer, and cook for 2 to 3 minutes, or until the bottoms are light golden in color.

7 Carefully pour hot water into the pan. Cover, and increase the heat to medium-high. Cook until almost all the water has evaporated, about 6 to 8 minutes.

8 Uncover, and continue cooking until all the water evaporates. Gently loosen the pot stickers from the bottom of the pan with a spatula.

9 Cover the pan with a serving plate, and quickly turn the pan over so that the browned sides of the pot stickers are on top. Cover plate with foil while preparing remaining pot stickers.

10 Repeat with remaining oil and dumplings. Serve hot with the dipping sauce.

FOR DIPPING SAUCE

Blend all ingredients in a medium-sized bowl. Evenly divide among 8 individual bowls and serve with hot pot stickers.

DIPPING SAUCE

½ cup light soy sauce

½ cup rice vinegar

½ tablespoon finely shredded fresh ginger

¼ cup finely chopped scallion

¼ cup finely chopped garlic

OPPOSITE: Guests visit the China pavilion in World Showcase at EPCOT, 2021.

KALUA PORK SLIDERS WITH PINEAPPLE CHUTNEY AND SPICY MAYONNAISE

STARTERS & SMALL PLATES

Sweet brioche rolls, sweet-and-spicy pineapple chutney, and spicy mayo are perfect with the slow-roasted Kalua pork—give yourself plenty of time, as the pork needs to cook for 8 to 10 hours.

MAKES 14-16

INTRODUCED 2016 • HAWAI'I GLOBAL MARKETPLACE

KALUA PORK

1 (4-pound) boneless pork shoulder (or boneless pork butt)

Coarse salt and freshly ground black pepper, to taste

1 large organic banana leaf, cut in half widthwise, optional

FOR KALUA PORK

1 Cut pork into 2 pieces; season with salt and pepper and wrap each piece in a banana leaf half.

2 Place wrapped pork in a slow cooker. Cover and cook on lowest setting for 8 to 10 hours, until meat shreds easily with a fork.

3 Remove meat from slow cooker, reserving drippings. Discard banana leaf, if using. Shred meat, adding drippings as needed to moisten.

(RECIPE CONTINUES ON PAGE 134)

KALUA PORK SLIDERS WITH PINEAPPLE CHUTNEY AND SPICY MAYONNAISE

(CONTINUED)

FOR BRIOCHE ROLLS

1. Combine warm water and yeast in the bowl of an electric mixer fitted with a dough hook attachment. Stir to dissolve yeast. Then set aside for 5 minutes, until mixture begins to bubble slightly.

2. Add 3 whole eggs plus 2 additional egg yolks, pineapple, and sugar. Add 3½ cups flour and knead with dough hook until a dough forms. Add butter, kneading until dough is combined.

3. Add remaining 1 cup flour as needed, a bit at a time, until dough pulls away from sides of the bowl. (You may not use all remaining flour.)

4. With lightly floured hands, pull dough into pieces slightly larger than a golf ball. Roll into smooth balls, and place on baking sheet lined with parchment paper.

5. Cover with a clean kitchen towel; set aside in a warm place to rise until doubled in size, about 1 hour.

6. Preheat oven to 350°F. Whisk together 1 egg white and 2 tablespoons water. Brush on tops of rolls. If desired, repeat with the second egg white. Bake until deep golden brown, about 20 to 25 minutes.

FOR PINEAPPLE CHUTNEY

Combine all ingredients in a large saucepan over medium-high heat; bring to a boil. Lower heat to medium-low and simmer until pineapple starts falling apart and most of the liquid has evaporated, about 1½ to 2 hours.

BRIOCHE ROLLS

⅓ cup warm (110°F) water

½ teaspoon active dry yeast

3 eggs, whole

2 eggs, divided into yolks and whites

½ cup drained crushed pineapple

¼ cup sugar

3½–4½ cups all-purpose flour, divided

¾ cup unsalted butter, softened

2 tablespoons water, plus more as needed

FOR SPICY MAYONNAISE

Combine all ingredients in a small bowl, stirring until combined.

TO SERVE

Cut Brioche Rolls in half. Place warm pulled pork on bottom of roll. Place Pineapple Chutney on top and drizzle Spicy Mayonnaise over chutney. Top with second half of Brioche Roll.

PINEAPPLE CHUTNEY

1 pound diced pineapple

1 large sweet yellow onion, diced

½ small red bell pepper, diced small

¼ teaspoon hot red pepper flakes

1 cup rice vinegar

½ cup white vinegar

¼ cup brown sugar

1 tablespoon minced garlic

1 tablespoon finely grated fresh ginger

Coarse salt, to taste

SPICY MAYONNAISE

6 tablespoons mayonnaise

2 tablespoons Sriracha (hot chili-garlic sauce)

2 teaspoons white vinegar

Coarse salt, to taste

LEFT: Honoring the fiftieth anniversary of the Walt Disney World Resort, Spaceship Earth at EPCOT, shown here in 2022, is outfitted with more than 1,800 Points of Light, including the eleven thousand side-firing light beams that result in the iconic starburst effects.

BEEF EMPANADAS

STARTERS & SMALL PLATES

These savory turnovers were first served at the festival more than twenty years ago—in 2002 at the Argentina Global Marketplace. The trick is to cut the beef into very small pieces—leftover pot roast works well with this recipe. Store-bought pie crust dough works if you prefer to make just the filling.

MAKES 20

INTRODUCED 2006 • ARGENTINA GLOBAL MARKETPLACE

VEGETABLE SHORTENING DOUGH

6 cups all-purpose flour

1 tablespoon salt

½ pound cold vegetable shortening, cut into ¼-inch cubes

1 egg, beaten

1 cup ice water, divided

BEEF FILLING

½ cup melted vegetable shortening (or vegetable oil)

2 cups finely chopped white onion

1¼ pounds ground beef

1½ tablespoons paprika

1 tablespoon red pepper flakes

1 teaspoon coarse salt

½ teaspoon freshly ground black pepper

FOR VEGETABLE SHORTENING DOUGH

1. Combine the flour and salt in a large mixing bowl. With your fingers, work the vegetable shortening (or vegetable oil) into the flour until the mixture resembles coarse meal.

2. Combine egg with ¾ cup ice water; gradually add water mixture to flour mixture, and stir with a wooden spoon until a soft dough forms. Add up to ¼ cup ice water if dough seems dry.

3. Transfer the dough to a floured surface and knead 5 to 6 turns. Divide dough into 2 pieces, form each into a disk, and wrap each disk tightly with plastic wrap. Refrigerate for 30 minutes.

FOR BEEF FILLING

Heat the vegetable shortening (or vegetable oil) in a large sauté pan over medium heat. Add the onions, and cook until soft but not brown, about 10 minutes. Stir in the beef, paprika, red pepper flakes, salt, and pepper. Cook, stirring constantly, until the mixture is well combined, about 3 minutes. Let cool for 15 minutes.

FOR BEEF EMPANADAS

1 Preheat oven to 400°F. On a large, floured surface, roll out half of Vegetable Shortening Dough to ⅛-inch thickness. With a 5-inch round cutter, cut 10 circles. Repeat with remaining half of dough.

2 Add water to the egg. Lightly brush the outside edges of each circle with egg wash, and spoon about 2 tablespoons of Beef Filling in the centers.

3 Fold the dough in half, enclosing the filling, and firmly press the edges together. Press the tines of a fork along the edges to seal.

4 Place the empanadas on two ungreased baking sheets, and lightly brush the top of each with egg wash. Bake for 25 minutes, or until golden brown. Serve immediately with salsa, if desired.

BEEF EMPANADAS

All-purpose flour (reserved from Vegetable Shortening Dough)

Vegetable Shortening Dough

½ tablespoon water

1 egg, beaten

Beef Filling

Favorite salsa, optional for serving

FILET OF BEEF WITH ROASTED MUSHROOMS AND TRUFFLE BEURRE BLANC

A perennial festival favorite, the buttery filet gets a drizzle of rich truffle beurre blanc and roasted mushrooms.

SERVES 4

INTRODUCED 2012 • CANADA GLOBAL MARKETPLACE

FOR TRUFFLE BEURRE BLANC

1. Sauté shallot in the extra-virgin olive oil in a sauté pan over medium heat until translucent. Add white wine and cook until it evaporates. Add cream and reduce to about ¼ cup.

2. Remove from heat and whisk in butter and truffle oil. Season with salt and pepper; add lemon juice, to taste. Strain through a fine-mesh strainer. Stir in chives and keep warm.

FOR ROASTED MUSHROOMS

Preheat oven to 375°F. Toss mushrooms with extra-virgin olive oil. Add garlic, and season with salt and pepper. Then place on parchment-lined sheet pan, and roast for 20 minutes. Remove from oven and set aside.

TRUFFLE BEURRE BLANC

1 shallot, sliced

1 tablespoon extra-virgin olive oil

1 cup white wine

1 cup heavy cream

¼ cup unsalted butter, cubed

1 tablespoon truffle oil

Coarse salt and freshly ground black pepper, to taste

Fresh lemon juice, to taste

1 tablespoon finely minced chives

ROASTED MUSHROOMS

½ pound button or mini portobello mushrooms, cleaned and sliced

2 tablespoon extra-virgin olive oil

1 tablespoon minced garlic

Coarse salt and freshly ground black pepper, to taste

FOR FILET OF BEEF

Preheat oven to 350°F. Season beef on all sides with salt and pepper. Heat canola oil in a large sauté pan or skillet over medium-high heat. Add steaks and sear, about 2 minutes each side. Transfer steaks to an ovenproof baking dish and place in oven for about 5 minutes for medium-rare.

TO SERVE

While steaks are in oven, add mushrooms to sauté pan and stir over medium heat for 2 to 3 minutes. Top steaks with mushrooms and 2 tablespoons of beurre blanc sauce. Serve immediately.

FILET OF BEEF

4 (6-ounce) filet mignons

Coarse salt and freshly ground black pepper, to taste

1 tablespoon canola oil

GRILLED LAMB CHOP WITH MINT PESTO AND POTATO CRUNCHIES

Salt and vinegar potato chips on a beautiful lamb chop? It's a match made in heaven. Start with a drizzle of mint pesto with feta cheese, then top with crushed chips. It's a surprising finish your dinner guests will love.

SERVES 4

INTRODUCED 2015 • AUSTRALIA GLOBAL MARKETPLACE

FOR MINT PESTO

1. Place garlic, ½ teaspoon salt, and ¼ cup olive oil into a blender or food processor. Blend to a paste.

2. Gradually add mint leaves and pulse until emulsified. Gradually add remaining oil.

3. Adjust seasoning with remaining salt, as needed. Refrigerate until ready to serve. Mix in feta cheese just before serving.

FOR GRILLED LAMB CHOPS

Combine olive oil, pepper, and salt in a shallow dish large enough to place the lamb chops in a single layer. Coat both sides of chops with oil. Then grill lamb chops, uncovered, over medium heat for 10 to 15 minutes, turning once, or until desired doneness.

TO SERVE

Spread 1 tablespoon Mint Pesto on each Grilled Lamb Chop. Evenly top each with a sprinkle of crushed potato chips. Refrigerate remaining pesto in sealed container.

MINT PESTO

2 cloves garlic, minced

1 teaspoon coarse salt, divided

¾ cup olive oil, divided

¼ cup mint leaves, washed and dried

¼ cup crumbled feta cheese

GRILLED LAMB CHOPS

¼ cup olive oil

¼ teaspoon freshly ground black pepper

¼ teaspoon coarse salt

4 Australian lamb chops

⅓ cup crushed salt and vinegar potato chips, for serving

RED CURRY CHICKEN

Once you gather the spices, this recipe comes together quickly in one pot with a side of basmati or jasmine rice.

SERVES 6

**INTRODUCED 2015 • INDIA
GLOBAL MARKETPLACE**

1 Blend garlic and ginger root with ¼ cup water in food processor or blender. Set aside.

2 Heat clarified butter (or vegetable oil) over medium heat in a heavy pot. Add cumin, cardamom, paprika, cayenne, coriander, bay leaves, salt, and pepper. Stir and cook until lightly browned, about 5 minutes, until spices become intense. Reduce heat if necessary to avoid burning.

3 Add onions and cook for about 5 minutes over medium heat until caramelized, stirring often. Add garlic and ginger mixture, and cook for 5 minutes. Remove bay leaves and larger pieces of cardamom pods.

4 Combine 2¾ cups water with tomato paste in a small bowl. Blend thoroughly and whisk into pot with other ingredients.

5 Add chicken and bring to a boil over medium-high heat. Reduce heat and simmer 10 minutes or until chicken is heated through. Stir in garam masala and sour cream. Top with cilantro and serve over basmati or jasmine rice.

10 cloves garlic

2 (2 × 1-inch) fresh ginger root pieces, peeled

3 cups water, divided

½ cup clarified butter, aka ghee (or vegetable oil)

2 teaspoons ground cumin

10 cardamom pods, lightly crushed

½ cup paprika

1 teaspoon ground cayenne pepper

2 teaspoons ground coriander

6 bay leaves

1 teaspoon salt

1 tablespoon freshly ground black pepper

1 large Spanish onion, coarsely chopped

2 (6-ounce) cans tomato paste

2 pounds cooked chicken thighs (about 10 medium thighs), meat cut in 1½-inch pieces or strips

2 tablespoons garam masala

1 cup sour cream

1 cup coarsely chopped fresh cilantro

Basmati or jasmine rice, cooked, for serving

BUTTER CHICKEN

Butter chicken is always a crowd pleaser—even more so when served with warm naan. Add a little extra ginger, chili powder, and cayenne for more heat in the sauce. Pair with a bold South African chenin blanc.

SERVES 4-6

INTRODUCED 2016 • AFRICA GLOBAL MARKETPLACE

FOR BUTTER SAUCE

1 Heat canola oil in a large saucepan over medium heat. Add onions and green pepper and sauté 3 to 5 minutes, or until soft.

2 Add butter, lemon juice, garlic paste, ginger paste, garam masala, chili powder, cumin, bay leaves, and cayenne pepper. Stir 1 to 2 minutes. Then add tomato purée, and cook 2 minutes, stirring frequently.

3 Reduce to low heat, and add cream and yogurt. Simmer 8 to 10 minutes. Then remove bay leaves, and season with salt and pepper. Set aside and keep warm.

BUTTER SAUCE

1 tablespoon canola oil

½ cup diced onion

½ cup diced green pepper

2 tablespoons unsalted butter

1 tablespoon lemon juice

1 teaspoon garlic paste

1 teaspoon ginger paste

1¼ teaspoons garam masala

1¼ teaspoons chili powder

1¼ teaspoons ground cumin

2 bay leaves

½ teaspoon cayenne pepper

1 cup tomato purée

1 cup heavy cream

⅓ cup plain yogurt

Coarse salt and freshly ground black pepper, to taste

LEFT: Guests walk toward the radiant Spaceship Earth at EPCOT, 2021.

FOR BUTTER CHICKEN

1. Combine garam masala and cayenne pepper in a bowl large enough to hold chicken. Toss with chicken until evenly coated; set aside.

2. Heat canola oil in a large sauté pan over medium-high heat. Add chicken and sauté 5 minutes until browned.

3. Lower heat to medium-low and stir in ½ cup Butter Sauce; simmer 3 to 5 minutes, or until chicken is thoroughly cooked. Stir in remaining sauce.

4. Mix cornstarch and chicken broth together in a small bowl. Stir into chicken and simmer 5 minutes, or until sauce thickens. Season with salt and pepper.

TO SERVE

Serve over rice with warm naan bread.

BUTTER CHICKEN

4 teaspoons garam masala

1 teaspoon ground cayenne pepper

2 pounds boneless, skinless chicken thighs, cut into bite-size pieces

1 tablespoon canola oil

Butter Sauce

1 tablespoon cornstarch

¼ cup chicken broth

Coarse salt and freshly ground black pepper, to taste

Basmati or jasmine rice, cooked for serving

Naan bread, for serving

CHICKEN TIKKA MASALA

Marinating the diced chicken for 10 to 12 hours creates a tender, flavorful dish. Pile in warm naan for the ultimate messy comfort food.

SERVES 4

INTRODUCED 2022 • INDIA GLOBAL MARKETPLACE

FOR MARINATED CHICKEN

Trim fat from chicken thighs and dice into ½-inch cubes. Combine remaining ingredients in a large bowl. Add chicken thighs and stir until chicken is coated. Cover and refrigerate 8 to 12 hours.

FOR FENNEL-SPICED YOGURT

Place Greek yogurt, ground fennel, salt, and pepper in a small mixing bowl. Stir to combine. Season with additional salt and pepper, if desired. Cover and refrigerate until ready to serve.

MARINATED CHICKEN

2 pounds boneless, skinless chicken thighs

1 cup Greek yogurt

1 teaspoon chopped garlic

1 teaspoon chopped fresh ginger

1 teaspoon garam masala

½ teaspoon ground turmeric

1 teaspoon ground cumin

1 teaspoon chili powder

2 teaspoons salt

⅛ teaspoon freshly ground black pepper

FENNEL-SPICED YOGURT

1 cup Greek yogurt

1 teaspoon ground fennel seed

½ teaspoon coarse salt, plus more to taste

Freshly ground black pepper, to taste

FOR CHICKEN TIKKA MASALA

1 Heat 1½ tablespoons canola oil in a medium-sized saucepan over medium heat for 5 minutes, until hot. Remove chicken thighs from marinade and sauté for 5 to 8 minutes, until fully cooked. Turn off heat and transfer chicken to a plate.

2 Add remaining 1½ tablespoons canola oil and the butter to the same saucepan. Cook over medium heat until butter is melted. Add onions and garlic and cook for 3 to 5 minutes, until fragrant. Stir in cayenne, garam masala, turmeric, and chili powder and cook, stirring often, for 5 minutes.

3 Add diced tomatoes and tomato paste and stir to combine. Bring to a simmer, then reduce heat to low and simmer for 20 minutes. Add heavy cream and brown sugar and simmer for an additional 15 minutes. Return chicken to pan and cook for 5 minutes. Season with salt and pepper, to taste. Keep warm until ready to serve.

FOR GARLIC NAAN

Preheat oven to 350°F. Place naan on a large baking sheet. Mix softened butter, garlic, and cilantro in a medium-sized bowl. Then brush (or spread) butter on top of each naan, and bake for 6 minutes, until warm and slightly crispy on edges.

TO SERVE

Place Chicken Tikka Masala in a bowl. Top with 2 tablespoons of Fennel-Spiced Yogurt. Serve with warm Garlic Naan.

CHICKEN TIKKA MASALA

3 tablespoons canola oil, divided

Marinated Chicken

½ cup unsalted butter

2 cups diced white onion

2 tablespoons minced garlic

Pinch ground cayenne pepper

1 teaspoon garam masala

1 teaspoon ground turmeric

1 teaspoon chili powder

1 (15-ounce) can diced tomatoes

1 tablespoon tomato paste

1 cup heavy cream

2 tablespoons brown sugar

Coarse salt and freshly ground black pepper, to taste

GARLIC NAAN

4 plain naan flatbreads

½ cup salted butter, softened

1 tablespoon chopped garlic

1 teaspoon finely chopped fresh cilantro

VERLASSO® SALMON WITH QUINOA SALAD AND ARUGULA CHIMICHURRI

MAINS & SIDES

Chimichurri made with peppery arugula adds a nice burst of flavor to the buttery salmon, with a protein-rich quinoa salad on the side. Verlasso® salmon are sustainable, farm-raised fish from Patagonia. Try pairing with Chile's medium-bodied Cono Sur Bicicleta Viognier.

SERVES 6

INTRODUCED 2015 · ARGENTINA GLOBAL MARKETPLACE

VERLASSO® SALMON

1 teaspoon garlic salt

¼ cup lemon juice

¼ cup olive oil

6 (5- to 6-ounce) Verlasso® salmon fillets, skin removed

ARUGULA CHIMICHURRI

1 cup coarsely chopped fresh cilantro (chopped from half of a bunch, including stems)

2 cups coarsely chopped fresh arugula

½ cup olive oil

¼ cup packed fresh mint leaves

3 tablespoons lime juice

½ teaspoon crushed red pepper flakes

1 teaspoon minced garlic

1 tablespoon red wine vinegar

Coarse salt and freshly ground black pepper, to taste

FOR VERLASSO® SALMON

1 Combine garlic salt, lemon juice, and olive oil in a small bowl. Place salmon in a large zip-top bag and add liquid, turning fillets to evenly coat.

2 Refrigerate for 30 minutes. Remove salmon from refrigerator at least 10 minutes before cooking.

3 Preheat oven to 400°F. Cover a 15 × 10-inch baking sheet with aluminum foil and lightly spray with nonstick cooking spray. Place salmon on baking sheet in a single layer, evenly spaced.

4 Bake 15 minutes or until the salmon easily can be flaked apart with a fork.

FOR ARUGULA CHIMICHURRI

Place all ingredients in blender or food processor. Blend for about 10 seconds on medium speed or until ingredients are evenly mixed. Season with salt and pepper. Store in a sealed container and refrigerate until ready to use.

QUINOA SALAD DRESSING

½ cup olive oil

¼ cup lime juice

1 teaspoon minced garlic

1 teaspoon white wine vinegar

¼ teaspoon ground cumin

Coarse salt and freshly ground black pepper, to taste

QUINOA SALAD

¾ cup uncooked quinoa, cooked per instructions, then cooled (approximately 3 cups cooked)

½ red pepper, diced

½ green pepper, diced

½ red onion, diced

1 small tomato, diced

¼ cup corn kernels

¼ cup finely chopped fresh cilantro

Coarse salt and freshly ground black pepper, to taste

FOR QUINOA SALAD DRESSING

Whisk all ingredients together in a small bowl. Season with salt and pepper. Set aside.

FOR QUINOA SALAD

Mix all ingredients together in a large bowl and toss with Quinoa Salad Dressing.

TO SERVE

Equally divide Quinoa Salad among serving plates, top with salmon fillet, and drizzle with chimichurri sauce.

STEAMED MUSSELS IN ROASTED GARLIC CREAM

This recipe debuted way back in 2010 at the Belgium Marketplace—since steamed mussels are considered the national dish of Belgium. Use a discarded shell to sip this silky roasted garlic cream.

SERVES 6

INTRODUCED 2010 • BELGIUM GLOBAL MARKETPLACE

ROASTED GARLIC PURÉE

1 large head garlic

1 tablespoon olive oil

ROASTED GARLIC CREAM

1 tablespoon olive oil

2 shallots, minced

½ cup white wine

1 tablespoon lemon juice

2 cups heavy cream

2 tablespoons Roasted Garlic Purée

½ teaspoon coarse salt

¼ teaspoon freshly ground black pepper

FOR ROASTED GARLIC PURÉE

1. Preheat oven to 350°F. Remove excess papery skin from garlic, keeping head intact. Cut top quarter off garlic head, exposing the cloves.

2. Place each head of garlic cut side up on an individual square of aluminum foil. Drizzle with oil. Wrap in foil, sealing edges.

3. Place the in oven and roast for 45 minutes. Cool for 20 minutes or until cool enough to handle.

4. Squeeze garlic cloves from skins into a small bowl. Discard skins. Mash garlic with a fork until smooth.

FOR ROASTED GARLIC CREAM

1. Heat oil in a medium-sized saucepan over medium heat. Add shallots and cook until softened, about 3 minutes. Add wine and lemon juice, stirring to combine. Cook until reduced by half, stirring occasionally, about 5 minutes.

2. Add cream, Roasted Garlic Purée, salt, and pepper, whisking to combine. Simmer (do not boil) until sauce is slightly thickened, about 4 to 5 minutes. Set aside.

FOR STEAMED MUSSELS

1. Place mussels, wine, and water in a large stockpot over high heat. Cover and bring to a boil.

2. Cook until mussels open, about 4 minutes. Remove and discard any mussels that do not open. Strain cooking liquid from mussels and discard liquid.

3. Place mussels in a large serving bowl, or in individual shallow bowls. Pour Roasted Garlic Cream over mussels, and top with parsley, dill, and chives. Serve immediately with toasted bread.

STEAMED MUSSELS

4 pounds fresh mussels, scrubbed and debearded

1 cup dry white wine

1 cup water

Roasted Garlic Cream

2 teaspoons chopped fresh parsley

2 teaspoons chopped fresh dill

2 teaspoons chopped fresh chives

4 thick slices sourdough bread, toasted

ABOVE, BOTTOM: Marquee installations for the EPCOT International Food & Wine Festival from 2017 (left) and 2018 (right).

EPCOT INTERNATIONAL FOOD & WINE FESTIVAL · WALT DISNEY WORLD

MOQUECA FISH STEW WITH COCONUT MILK

MAINS & SIDES

Start with the freshest fish you can find for this creamy, rich stew with a base of garlic, onions, and peppers, flavored with coconut milk. If you prefer, fresh shrimp is a delicious stand-in for fish. Sip Brazil's light, refreshing Xingu Black Beer (pronounced "shin-goo"), with hints of chocolate and roasted malts.

SERVES 4–6

INTRODUCED 2015 • BRAZIL GLOBAL MARKETPLACE

1 Heat 1 tablespoon extra-virgin olive oil in a nonstick sauté pan over medium-high heat. Add fish fillets, searing on both sides until almost cooked through. Remove fish with a slotted spoon and transfer to a plate; tent loosely with foil and set aside.

2 Add remaining 1 tablespoon oil to pan over medium heat. Add onions, garlic, poblano pepper, and red bell pepper, and sauté until softened, about 3 minutes.

3 Add tomato paste, stirring to combine. Add 1 tablespoon cilantro, ¼ teaspoon salt, and paprika.

4 Add fish stock, clam juice, or vegetable broth, stirring until well combined. Bring to a boil over high heat. Lower heat to medium. Add coconut milk and simmer 10 minutes.

5 Add tomatoes, hearts of palm, and lemon juice, stirring to combine. Season with salt and pepper.

6 Return fish to stew, stirring gently to combine. Simmer 30 seconds. Sprinkle with remaining cilantro. Serve over rice.

2 tablespoons extra-virgin olive oil, divided

1 pound mild white fish fillets (such as snapper, grouper, or mahi-mahi)

1 small onion, chopped

4 large garlic cloves, minced

½ cup chopped poblano pepper

⅓ cup chopped red bell pepper

1 teaspoon tomato paste

2 tablespoons finely chopped fresh cilantro, divided

¼ teaspoon coarse salt, plus more to taste

⅛ teaspoon paprika

1 cup fish stock, clam juice, or low-sodium vegetable broth

1 cup coconut milk

3 plum tomatoes, seeded and diced

⅓ cup canned hearts of palm, drained and diced

1 tablespoon fresh lemon juice

Freshly ground black pepper, to taste

Cooked white rice, for serving

SEAFOOD FISHERMAN'S PIE

A perennial festival favorite, this dish takes time and attention, but the end result is a rich seafood supper with shrimp, scallops, lobster bisque, and a topping of creamy mashed potatoes finished with Irish Cheddar cheese. The bisque base uses only the lobster shells, so you could substitute lobster for the shrimp in the pie. Nice with a Napa Valley chardonnay.

SERVES 8

INTRODUCED 2016 • IRELAND GLOBAL MARKETPLACE

FOR LOBSTER BISQUE

1 Place butter and olive oil in a large, heavy-bottomed saucepan over medium heat. Sauté onions, celery, and fennel for 6 to 7 minutes, or until tender. Add lobster shells and tomato purée and continue to cook for 1 to 2 minutes. Add flour and stir until combined; cook another 1 to 2 minutes.

2 Add cognac and stock and simmer for 30 minutes, stirring and scraping bottom of pan with a wooden spoon to loosen any brown bits.

3 Add cream and bring to a boil; lower heat and simmer for 15 minutes. Stir in cayenne, garlic, and chervil.

4 Remove lobster shells and place mixture in blender; blend on medium speed for 15 to 20 seconds, or until smooth. Scrape sides and blend another 5 seconds.

5 Pour bisque through a fine strainer lined with cheesecloth to remove shell pieces.

6 Pour bisque back into saucepan over medium heat and return to a boil. Season with salt and pepper. Set aside.

LOBSTER BISQUE

2 tablespoons unsalted butter

2 tablespoons olive oil

1½ cups chopped onion

2 cups chopped celery

1½ cups chopped fennel

2 lobster shells, meat removed

½ cup tomato purée

2 tablespoons flour

1 tablespoon cognac

4 cups fish or chicken stock

2 cups heavy whipping cream

¼ teaspoon ground cayenne pepper

1 teaspoon crushed garlic

1 teaspoon chervil

½ teaspoon coarse salt

¼ teaspoon freshly ground black pepper

FOR MASHED POTATOES

1 Place potatoes in a large stockpot of lightly salted boiling water over high heat for 15 to 20 minutes or until the potatoes are soft.

2 Drain and then whip potatoes with an electric hand mixer on low speed. Stir in butter and cream or milk. Season with salt and pepper. Set aside, and keep warm until ready to serve.

FOR FISHERMAN'S PIE

1 Preheat oven to 350°F. Place butter and olive oil in a large stockpot over medium heat. Sauté onions, celery, and carrot for 6 to 7 minutes or until tender. Add flour and stir until combined, cooking 1 to 2 minutes.

2 Add brandy and stir for 1 to 2 minutes. Stir in shrimp, scallops, Lobster Bisque, and tarragon. Continue to cook 8 to 10 minutes or until mixture boils. Add hot pepper sauce, and season with salt and pepper.

3 Pour mixture into 3-quart baking dish. Evenly spread Mashed Potatoes on top, covering entire dish. Top with cheese. Bake 25 minutes, or until bubbling and cheese melts.

MASHED POTATOES

4–6 large potatoes, peeled and cubed

¼ cup unsalted butter

½ cup heavy whipping cream or milk

Coarse salt and freshly ground black pepper, to taste

FISHERMAN'S PIE

2 tablespoons unsalted butter

1 tablespoon olive oil

1 cup diced onion

1 cup diced celery

1 cup diced carrot

3½ tablespoons flour

2 tablespoons brandy

1 pound fresh shrimp, deveined

1 pound bay scallops

4 cups Lobster Bisque

½ teaspoon tarragon

⅛ teaspoon hot pepper sauce

Coarse salt and freshly ground black pepper, to taste

Mashed Potatoes

2 cups shredded Irish Cheddar cheese

ONION TART

Sweet caramelized onions are the star of this tart that is perfect for brunch, lunch, or dinner. And it's even better the next day. A French pinot gris counters the creaminess of this dish.

SERVES 4

INTRODUCED 2015 • FRANCE GLOBAL MARKETPLACE

2 tablespoons unsalted butter

2 tablespoons olive oil

1 pound yellow onions, thinly sliced

1 teaspoon coarse salt

1 sheet puff pastry, thawed

2 eggs

2 tablespoons heavy cream

1. Preheat oven to 400°F. Heat butter and olive oil in a large sauté pan over medium-high heat. Add onions and salt, stirring to combine. Cook 25 to 30 minutes, or until onions are golden and caramelized. Set aside to cool.

2. As onions cool, roll pastry into a 12-inch square on a lightly floured surface. Brush edges with water and fold, creating a 1½-inch border. Press lightly with a fork to seal. Prick center of dough with a fork 15 times.

3. Place dough on a parchment-lined baking sheet. Bake pastry for 8 minutes.

4. In a large bowl, whisk together eggs and cream. Add cooled onions, stirring to combine. Carefully transfer onion-egg mixture to the center of the par-baked pastry. Return tart to oven and bake for 15 minutes. Cool before slicing.

MAI TAI

A taste of the islands, though the drink is said to have been first concocted in California in the 1940s during the tiki bar craze.

SERVES 1

INTRODUCED 2015 • HAWAI'I GLOBAL MARKETPLACE

1½ ounces rum

2½ ounces pineapple juice

½ ounce mango purée

¼ ounce fresh lime juice

1 cup ice

Fresh pineapple wedge

Pour rum, pineapple juice, mango purée, and lime juice into shaker. Fill with ice and vigorously shake for 30 seconds. Strain into a double rocks glass filled with ice, and top with pineapple wedge.

ABOVE: Guests wander World Showcase during the 2019 EPCOT International Food & Wine Festival.

TROPICAL MIMOSAS

Give your next brunch an upgrade with this bubbly cocktail. You can combine champagne (preferably a brut) or a dry prosecco with any juice—just mix it 1:1. Other favorites: pomegranate juice, grapefruit juice, or pear nectar.

3 ounces orange juice

3 ounces passion fruit juice

3 ounces guava juice

9 ounces prosecco

SERVES 4

INTRODUCED 2018 • SHIMMERING SIPS MIMOSA BAR GLOBAL MARKETPLACE

1 Rinse and chill champagne flutes in freezer to frost glasses. Mix together orange juice, passion fruit juice, and guava juice.

2 Remove flutes from freezer and fill halfway with mixed juice. Fill to the rim with prosecco.

EPCOT INTERNATIONAL FOOD & WINE FESTIVAL · WALT DISNEY WORLD

SOJU SLUSHY

MOCKTAILS & COCKTAILS

Soju is a Korean liquor that's stronger than beer or wine, but with much less alcohol than vodka. Smooth and mild, it will mix with your favorite fruit flavors!

SERVES 1

INTRODUCED 2013 • SOUTH KOREA GLOBAL MARKETPLACE

Soju

1½ ounces orange, guava, and passion fruit frozen concentrate

½ ounce lime juice

1 cup ice

Orange slice, for serving

Combine liquor, frozen concentrate, lime juice, and ice in blender, and blend until smooth. Pour into a glass, and top with orange slice.

PUMPKIN CHAI TEA AND CARAMEL MILKSHAKE

Start with flavors of pumpkin and chai, then add vanilla ice cream and sweet caramel syrup for a shareable sweet. For a grown-up version, add two ounces of caramel vodka while blending, or just pour over the top before serving.

6 tablespoons hot water

1 pumpkin spice chai tea bag

16 ounces vanilla ice cream

2 tablespoons caramel syrup

1 tablespoon shortbread cookie crumbles, for serving

SERVES 2

INTRODUCED 2016 • IRELAND GLOBAL MARKETPLACE

1 Pour hot water into a heatproof container. Steep tea bag in hot water for 3 minutes. Then squeeze tea bag and remove. Chill tea.

2 Place ice cream, chilled tea, and caramel syrup in a blender, and blend until smooth. Pour into serving glass, and top with shortbread cookie crumbles. Serve immediately.

EPCOT INTERNATIONAL FOOD & WINE FESTIVAL · WALT DISNEY WORLD

WARM CHOCOLATE LAVA CAKE WITH IRISH CREAM GANACHE

SWEET ENDINGS & DESSERTS

A favorite at the Ireland Marketplace! The sauce has changed over the years, including this version with Baileys® Original Irish Cream. Be careful not to overbake, so that the center remains molten.

SERVES 6

INTRODUCED 2002 • IRELAND GLOBAL MARKETPLACE

FOR IRISH CREAM GANACHE

Stir together cream and Irish cream in a small saucepan over medium heat. Just before boiling point, remove from heat and stir in milk chocolate.

FOR WARM CHOCOLATE LAVA CAKE

1. Preheat oven to 425°F. Lightly butter sides of 6 individual (¾-cup) ramekins. Coat with sugar, then shake out excess.

2. Melt chocolate and butter in top of double boiler set over simmering water, stirring until smooth. Remove from heat and cool 10 minutes.

3. Beat egg yolks and whole eggs together in a large bowl; add sugar and beat until thick and light, about 2 minutes. Then fold in chocolate mixture. Sift flour, then fold into batter, mixing until smooth.

4. Divide batter among prepared ramekins, filling each three-quarters full. Place on baking sheet and bake about 15 minutes or until sides of cake are firm but the middle is soft. Do not overbake.

5. Using a small knife, cut around sides of cakes to loosen. Let sit 1 minute, then invert onto plates and drizzle with ganache.

IRISH CREAM GANACHE

¼ cup heavy cream

¼ cup Irish cream, Baileys® Original Irish Cream preferred

4 ounces milk chocolate

WARM CHOCOLATE LAVA CAKE

8 (1-ounce) semisweet chocolate squares, chopped; or 1 cup semisweet chocolate chips

1 cup unsalted butter

5 egg yolks

4 whole eggs

¾ cup sugar

⅓ cup all-purpose flour

WARM CARROT CAKES WITH CREAM CHEESE ICING

Cranberries soaked in orange juice stand in for raisins in this classic cake that's sweetened with pineapple and topped with a tangy cream cheese frosting.

MAKES 12 SMALL CAKES

INTRODUCED 2014 • HOPS AND BARLEY GLOBAL MARKETPLACE

FOR WARM CARROT CAKES

1. Soak dried cranberries in orange juice overnight. When ready, preheat oven to 325°F, and butter and flour 12 (½-cup) oven-safe ramekins. Then combine sugar, vegetable oil, and eggs in the bowl of an electric mixer fitted with a paddle attachment; beat until light yellow. Stir in vanilla extract.

2. Sift together 2½ cups flour, cinnamon, baking soda, and salt in a medium-sized bowl. Add flour mixture to sugar-egg mixture until just combined.

3. Drain dried cranberries (discard any remaining orange juice). Toss cranberries and walnuts with 1 tablespoon flour. Add carrots and pineapple, tossing to combine. Fold mixture into batter. When ready, ladle batter into prepared ramekins. Bake 35 to 40 minutes, or until a toothpick inserted into cakes comes out clean.

FOR CREAM CHEESE ICING

Beat cream cheese and butter with an electric mixer until smooth. Beat in 1½ cups powdered sugar and vanilla extract. Add more powdered sugar and milk, 1 tablespoon at a time, until consistency is spreadable. While cakes are still warm, turn out of ramekins and spread with icing.

WARM CARROT CAKES

1 cup dried cranberries

1 cup orange juice

2 cups sugar

1⅓ cups vegetable oil

3 large eggs, room temperature

1 teaspoon vanilla extract

2½ cups plus 1 tablespoon all-purpose flour, divided

2 teaspoons ground cinnamon

2 teaspoons baking soda

1½ teaspoons coarse salt

1 cup chopped walnuts

2 cups grated carrots

½ cup diced fresh pineapple

CREAM CHEESE ICING

8 ounces cream cheese, softened

½ cup unsalted butter, softened

1½–2 cups powdered sugar, divided

½ teaspoon vanilla extract

1–3 tablespoons milk

OPPOSITE, BOTTOM: The main gate display for 2015 EPCOT International Food & Wine Festival.

APPLE STRUDEL

SWEET ENDINGS & DESSERTS

A classic at the festival, this recipe was added by Disney Culinary Director Christine Weissman, a native of Bielefeld, Germany. Phyllo dough can be tricky—if it cracks or tears, just trim and put another sheet on top.

SERVES 6

INTRODUCED 2012 • GERMANY GLOBAL MARKETPLACE

3 medium Granny Smith apples, peeled and thinly sliced

¼ cup raisins

¼ cup sugar

¼ teaspoon ground cinnamon

¼ cup plain bread crumbs

8 ounces (about 20 sheets) phyllo dough, thawed

¾ cup unsalted butter, melted

1 cup heavy cream, slightly whipped, optional

1 Preheat oven to 400°F. Gently mix apples, raisins, sugar, and cinnamon in a medium-sized bowl; set aside.

2 Toast bread crumbs in a small sauté pan over medium heat. Stir constantly until golden brown, about 5 minutes. Transfer to a small bowl and let cool.

3 Place a kitchen towel on a large work surface. Spread one sheet of phyllo dough on the kitchen towel and lightly brush the entire surface with melted butter. Layer another sheet on top, butter, and continue the process until all sheets are stacked. Then sprinkle the toasted bread crumbs along the longest side of the top sheet of buttered phyllo dough. Spread apple mixture on top of the bread crumbs.

4 Roll the strudel, jelly roll fashion, using the towel to help shape the dough, starting from the apple mixture side and continuing across. While rolling, make sure that apples do not spill from the ends. Place seam side down on baking sheet and brush with remaining melted butter.

5 Using a large spatula, place strudel on an ungreased baking sheet. Bake approximately 25 to 30 minutes or until the dough is golden brown.

6 Let cool at room temperature for 30 to 45 minutes. Slice strudel with a serrated knife into 6 portions; top with whipped cream, if desired.

OPPOSITE, TOP: Kids taste Apple Strudel and other treats at the Germany pavilion during the 2019 EPCOT International Food & Wine Festival.

BELGIAN WAFFLES WITH BERRY COMPOTE AND WHIPPED CREAM

SWEET ENDINGS & DESSERTS

Belgian waffles in some form or fashion make an appearance at every EPCOT International Food & Wine Festival. You can use any seasonal berry to top these light and crispy waffles, or go savory with bacon and eggs, fried chicken or ham and melted cheese. If you serve these waffles for an extravagant dessert, pour a glass of Moscato d'Asti from Italy.

MAKES 8 (4 × 4-INCH) WAFFLES TO SERVE 4

INTRODUCED 2016 • BELGIUM GLOBAL MARKETPLACE

BERRY COMPOTE

1 tablespoon cornstarch

1 tablespoon red wine

½ cup apple, orange, or cranberry juice

¼ cup sugar

1 teaspoon fresh lemon juice

1 cup fresh blueberries

1 cup fresh blackberries

1 cup chopped fresh strawberries

1 cup fresh raspberries

FOR BERRY COMPOTE

1 Combine cornstarch and red wine in a small bowl, stirring until cornstarch is dissolved. Set aside.

2 Combine fruit juice, sugar, and lemon juice in a small saucepan. Bring to a simmer. Add cornstarch mixture, blueberries, and blackberries.

3 Cook 1 to 2 minutes, until berries are softened and mixture is thickened. Add strawberries, stirring to combine. Remove from heat, and gently fold in raspberries. Serve warm over Belgian Waffles.

RIGHT: Guests take a moment to dance in the Italy pavilion in World Showcase at EPCOT, 2021.

FOR BELGIAN WAFFLES

1. Sift flour into a large bowl. Add sugar and yeast. Create a well in the center of the mixture.

2. Add water, milk, beer, egg, and vanilla extract. Stir until mixture is just blended. (Don't worry if there are lumps; they will dissolve as the batter rests overnight.)

3. Add melted butter, and stir until just incorporated. Refrigerate batter overnight.

4. Bring mixture to room temperature. Ladle waffle batter into a Belgian waffle maker; cook according to manufacturer's instructions.

5. Serve warm with Berry Compote and whipped cream.

BELGIAN WAFFLES

2½ cups all-purpose flour

2 tablespoons sugar

1 teaspoon dry active yeast

1½ cups water

½ cup milk

2 tablespoons beer

1 egg

1 tablespoon vanilla extract

½ cup unsalted butter, melted

Berry Compote, for serving

Whipped cream, for serving

CHAPTER FIVE
HOLIDAY MAGIC
at the Disneyland and Walt Disney World Resorts

THE WINTER HOLIDAYS are extra special at both the Walt Disney World Resort and the Disneyland Resort.

Colors, sights, sounds, and delicious dishes ring in the multicultural Lunar New Year at Disney California Adventure Park. Debuting in January 2013, the celebration now stretches to the Downtown Disney District and the hotels of the Disneyland Resort. Favorite Disney characters in Lunar New Year–inspired attire and Mulan's Lunar New Year Procession add an extra dose of joy.

Disney Festival of Holidays at Disney California Adventure Park became part of the winter festivities in 2016, a celebration of diverse cultural fun with a little taste of Christmas, Navidad, Hanukkah, Diwali, Kwanzaa, and Three Kings' Day Feast. Mickey Mouse and friends are part of the fun, with food and experiences for all ages.

Holidays Around the World got its start at EPCOT in 1994, when the legendary Candlelight Processional moved from the Magic Kingdom to the America Gardens Theatre. The name changed to EPCOT International Festival of the Holidays in 2017. You'll find plenty of holiday sweets and holiday dishes from around the globe, along with traditional celebrations in each of the World Showcase countries.

THESE PAGES: Festive moments to remember from Disney California Adventure at the Disneyland Resort: Mickey gingerbread (previous pages, 2021); a holiday tree at Carthay Circle (opposite, 2012); performers at the Disney ¡Viva Navidad! Street Party at Paradise Gardens (top and bottom, 2022); and Minnie Mouse at a Disney ¡Viva Navidad! character greeting pavilion (middle, 2022).

ABOVE, BOTTOM: The annual Lunar New Year Celebration at Disney California Adventure draws on Chinese and Vietnamese-inspired traditions. In 2022, to honor the Year of the Tiger from the Chinese zodiac calendar, guests could watch calligraphy artisans create cards with messages of hope for the New Year ahead.

PORK AND SHRIMP DUMPLINGS WITH BLACK GARLIC DIPPING SAUCE

MAINS & SIDES

Full of flavor and a hit at Lunar New Year, these dumplings take a while to prep but cook quickly and make enough to feed a crowd. Buy pork that contains 30 percent fat for the best results. They also are delicious as wontons served in a hot broth, and they freeze perfectly.

MAKES 40 DUMPLINGS

INTRODUCED 2023 • WRAPPED WITH LOVE FESTIVAL MARKETPLACE

FOR BLACK GARLIC DIPPING SAUCE

Use a fine grater to grate garlic into a paste. Whisk garlic paste with remaining ingredients in a large bowl. Refrigerate and use as dipping sauce or pour over dumplings.

FOR PORK AND SHRIMP DUMPLINGS

1 Combine pork, shrimp, sesame oil, ginger, garlic, green onions, salt, and pepper, mixing well.

2 Fill center of wonton wrapper with 1 tablespoon filling. Fold diagonally in half. Repeat until all filling is used. Place on parchment-lined baking sheet. Repeat with remaining filling and wrappers. (You can try other methods of folding the wrapper—just don't overfill.)

3 Place in bamboo steamer lined with cabbage leaves or parchment paper over a pot of boiling water, leaving space between dumplings. Cover tightly and steam until filling is firm and cooked through, 8 to 10 minutes. Repeat with remaining dumplings. Serve hot with Black Garlic Dipping Sauce.

BLACK GARLIC DIPPING SAUCE

1 clove black garlic

1 cup low-sodium soy sauce

1 cup rice vinegar

½ cup black vinegar

1 tablespoon agave

½ tablespoon sambal

1 tablespoon sliced green onion

PORK AND SHRIMP DUMPLINGS

½ pound ground pork

½ pound shrimp, finely minced

2 teaspoons sesame oil

1 teaspoon freshly grated ginger root

1 clove garlic, minced

2 green onions, thinly sliced

1½ teaspoons salt

½ teaspoon freshly ground black pepper

40 wonton wrappers

1 egg, beaten

SPICY PORK DAN DAN NOODLES

MAINS & SIDES

Tahini is the secret ingredient in the chili oil that adds a depth of flavor to the noodles, with guajillo and ancho chiles adding sweetness, and an árbol chile bringing the heat. You can substitute ground chicken for the pork, as the chili oil adds fat as it cooks with the meat.

SERVES 4-6

INTRODUCED 2022 • LONGEVITY NOODLE CO. FESTIVAL MARKETPLACE

FOR DAN DAN CHILI OIL

Pulse chiles into flakes in food processor. Place chiles and remaining ingredients in a medium-sized saucepan over medium heat, simmering until canola oil becomes fragrant. Remove from heat and cool completely.

FOR DAN DAN NOODLES

1. Cook pasta in boiling salted water according to package directions, and set aside. As pasta cooks, mix pork, Szechuan peppercorn, and salt in a small bowl.

2. Add Dan Dan Chili Oil to a large sauté pan over medium heat. Once oil is hot, add seasoned ground pork, breaking up meat with a wooden spoon. Cook until meat is crispy, then add bok choy and cook 2 to 3 minutes.

3. Drain pasta and add to pork and bok choy, tossing to coat noodles in sauce. Add remaining Dan Dan Chili Oil, if desired.

4. Divide noodles into serving dishes. Garnish with green onions and chopped peanuts.

DAN DAN CHILI OIL

2 dried guajillo chiles, deseeded

2 dried ancho chiles, deseeded

1 dried árbol chile

1 small shallot, peeled and minced

3 cloves garlic, peeled and minced

1 cup canola oil

½ cup tahini

1 teaspoon coarse salt

DAN DAN NOODLES

1 pound dried spaghetti

1 pound ground pork

½ teaspoon ground Szechuan peppercorn

1 teaspoon coarse salt

½ cup Dan Dan Chili Oil, plus more to taste

1 small bunch bok choy, washed and chopped

1 green onion, sliced

Chopped peanuts, for garnish

OPPOSITE, BOTTOM: For the 2022 Lunar New Year Celebration at Disney California Adventure, guests were invited to try activities throughout Paradise Gardens Park, ranging from coloring crafts (shown) to writing notes of health and happiness for the upcoming year to place on the Lucky Wishing Wall.

HOPPIN' JOHN WITH WHITE RICE AND CORNBREAD CRUMBLE

MAINS & SIDES

A classic Southern way to ring in the New Year, a bowlful is meant to bring good luck all year. The crumbled cornbread soaks up all the goodness.

SERVES 4

INTRODUCED 2016 • SEASONAL SOUTHERN DELIGHTS HOLIDAY KITCHEN

FOR CORNBREAD CRUMBLE

1. Preheat oven to 400°F. Spray an 8-inch square pan with nonstick cooking spray.

2. Combine melted butter, milk, and egg in a large bowl. Mix well. Add cornmeal, flour, sugar, baking powder, and salt to liquid ingredients. Stir until just moistened. Batter will be lumpy.

3. Allow cornbread batter to rest for 5 minutes. Then pour into prepared baking pan and spread evenly.

4. Bake for 20 to 25 minutes, until top is golden brown and a toothpick inserted into the center comes out clean.

5. Cool for 10 minutes, and then cut cornbread and crumble the pieces into a small bowl. Set aside.

CORNBREAD CRUMBLE

¼ cup unsalted butter or margarine, melted

1 cup milk

1 egg

1¼ cup cornmeal

1 cup all-purpose flour

½ cup sugar

1 tablespoon baking powder

½ teaspoon salt

LEFT: For the 2022 EPCOT International Festival of the Holidays, Disney Chefs created gingerbread lobby sculptures for The American Adventure pavilion in World Showcase at EPCOT. On display were the Lincoln Memorial, The American Adventure pavilion itself, and the *Stone of Hope* at the Martin Luther King, Jr. Memorial.

FOR HOPPIN' JOHN

1. Heat canola oil in a medium-sized saucepan over medium heat for 5 minutes, until hot. Add diced ham hock and cook 5 minutes, until browned.

2. Add onions, green pepper, and celery and sauté for 5 minutes, until onions begin to brown. Add garlic and cook for one additional minute.

3. Stir black-eyed peas, bay leaf, thyme, and chicken stock into saucepan. Add cayenne pepper, as well as salt and pepper, as needed.

4. Bring to a simmer and continue simmering, uncovered, for 40 minutes. Then stir in chopped kale.

5. To serve, divide rice into four bowls (about ½ cup in each). Spoon warm Hoppin' John over rice and top with Cornbread Crumble.

HOPPIN' JOHN

2 tablespoons canola oil

1 large smoked ham hock, diced

1 small onion, diced

1 green pepper, diced

1 celery stalk, diced

2 cloves garlic, minced

1 (15-ounce) can black-eyed peas, drained

1 bay leaf

1 teaspoon dried thyme

2 cups chicken stock

¼ teaspoon ground cayenne pepper

Coarse salt and freshly ground black pepper, to taste

2 cups chopped kale

Cooked white rice, for serving

PORK SCHNITZEL WITH MUSHROOM RAGOUT AND SPÄTZLE

Schnitzel is a simple way of preparing thin cutlets of meat, then breading and frying. Start with a boneless loin chop, sliced not too thick, not too thin, or ask your butcher to cut the chops to your desired thickness. The crispy pork schnitzel, spätzle, and Mushroom Ragout make a perfect bite.

SERVES 4   **INTRODUCED 2019 • BAVARIA HOLIDAY KITCHEN**

MUSHROOM RAGOUT

2 tablespoons extra-virgin olive oil

½ shallot, chopped

1 cloves garlic, minced

2 tablespoons unsalted butter

4 ounces sliced cremini mushrooms

4 ounces oyster mushrooms, trimmed and torn into smaller pieces

½ teaspoon chopped fresh rosemary

½ teaspoon chopped fresh thyme

½ teaspoon coarse salt, plus more to taste

1 tablespoon tomato paste

2 tablespoons all-purpose flour

1½ teaspoons red wine vinegar

¼ cup red wine

2 cups beef stock

¼ teaspoon freshly ground black pepper

FOR MUSHROOM RAGOUT

1. Heat extra-virgin olive oil in a large pot over medium heat for 5 minutes, until hot. Add shallot and cook, stirring often, for 3 to 5 minutes, until soft. Add garlic and cook for 30 seconds.

2. Add butter, mushrooms, rosemary, and thyme and cook for 7 minutes, until mushrooms begin to soften and reduce in size. Add salt and cook an additional 5 minutes.

3. Add tomato paste and flour and cook for 2 minutes, until flour is incorporated. Add red wine and vinegar and cook for 3 minutes. Pour in beef stock and increase heat to medium-high. Cook stirring frequently for 10 minutes, until ragout thickens and coats mushrooms.

4. Season with salt and pepper, to taste. Keep warm until ready to serve.

PORK SCHNITZEL

4 (½-inch thick) boneless pork chops

2 teaspoon coarse salt, divided

½ teaspoon freshly ground black pepper

1 cup all-purpose flour

2 large eggs, lightly beaten

1 cup plain bread crumbs

Canola oil, for frying

Minced chives, for serving

SPÄTZLE

1 (1-pound) pack uncooked spätzle

¼ cup unsalted butter

Coarse salt, to taste

Freshly ground nutmeg, to taste

FOR PORK SCHNITZEL

1 Place pork chops between 2 sheets of plastic wrap, and pound with meat mallet until ¼ inch thick. Lightly season pork with 1 teaspoon the salt and all the pepper.

2 Combine flour and remaining salt in a shallow bowl or pie plate. Place lightly beaten eggs in a second bowl and bread crumbs in a third bowl.

3 With caution, heat 1 inch of canola oil in a Dutch oven or large skillet over medium heat until it reaches 325°F.

4 Dip pork chops in flour mixture, then in eggs, and finally in bread crumbs. Carefully add to hot oil and cook for 2 to 3 minutes on each side, until golden brown. Drain on paper towels.

FOR SPÄTZLE

Cook spätzle according to package directions. Drain and set aside. Heat butter in a large sauté pan over medium heat until melted. Add spätzle and cook for 3 to 5 minutes, until golden brown. Season with salt and nutmeg, to taste.

TO SERVE

Place Spätzle in center of a plate. Cut Pork Schnitzel in half and place on top of Spätzle. Top with Mushroom Ragout and minced chives.

ABOVE: A close-up of the outdoor model village and railroad at the Germany pavilion in World Showcase at EPCOT, 2021.

SHREDDED BEEF TAMALE WITH AVOCADO CREMA

MAINS & SIDES

Making tamales for Christmas is a tradition for many Hispanic families, passed down for generations. The ultimate comfort food with slow-cooked beef, this is a recipe to enjoy year-round.

MAKES 12

INTRODUCED 2016 • FEAST OF THE THREE KINGS HOLIDAY KITCHEN

FOR SHREDDED BEEF FILLING

1. Place onions, tomatoes, peppers, and beef broth in the bottom of a slow cooker.

2. In a small bowl, mix garlic, tomato paste, onion powder, cumin, chili powder, dried oregano, coriander, cayenne pepper, and salt to form a paste.

3. Rub paste on all sides of the roast. Place in slow cooker. Cook on low for 8 hours, until beef shreds easily with a fork.

4. Shred the beef and stir with vegetables and liquid. Set aside to cool.

SHREDDED BEEF FILLING

1 medium onion, diced

1 (15-ounce) can diced tomatoes, drained

1 green bell pepper, diced

1 cup beef broth

2 cloves garlic, minced

2 tablespoons tomato paste

1 teaspoon onion powder

½ teaspoon ground cumin

½ teaspoon chili powder

1 teaspoon dried oregano

1½ teaspoons ground coriander

¼ teaspoon ground cayenne pepper

2 teaspoons coarse salt

2 pound beef chuck roast or brisket

THESE PAGES: The Candlelight Processional in World Showcase, an annual tradition of EPCOT International Festival of the Holidays, features a celebrity narrator sharing the story of Christmas, joined by massed choir members, shown here in 2021 (opposite, bottom; and page 181) and 2010 (right).

(RECIPE CONTINUES ON PAGE 180)

SHREDDED BEEF TAMALE WITH AVOCADO CREMA

(CONTINUED)

FOR TAMALES

1. Place corn husks in a large bowl. Cover with boiling water and soak for 2 hours. Drain and set aside.

2. Place masa flour, lard or vegetable shortening, salt, and baking powder in the bowl of an electric mixer fitted with a paddle attachment. Mix on low speed until lard is evenly distributed throughout the masa.

3. Add warm beef broth, ½ cup at a time, until mixture resembles smooth mashed potatoes.

4. Place one corn husk concave side up on a plate. Place 2 heaping tablespoons of the masa flour mix in the center of the corn husk. Press with fingers to evenly layer, keeping dough about ½ inch from the sides and 2 inches from the top and bottom of the corn husk.

5. Place one level tablespoon Shredded Beef Filling in the center of the dough. Bring the sides of the corn husk up to meet, pinching the dough to seal, then roll into a cylinder, folding the bottom and top toward the seam.

6. Place tamale seam side down in a steamer basket. Repeat with remaining corn husks, making sure not to have more than 2 layers of tamales.

7. Add a few inches of water to a large stock pot. Bring to a boil, then reduce to a simmer. Place steamer basket inside of pot. Steam tamales for 90 minutes, checking occasionally to see if more water is needed, until tamales start to separate from the corn husk. Set aside.

FOR CORN SALSA

Combine all ingredients in a medium-sized bowl, and then set aside.

TAMALES

12 dried corn husks

1¾ cups masa flour

¼ cup lard or vegetable shortening

½ tablespoon salt

¾ teaspoon baking powder

1–2 cups warm beef stock

CORN SALSA

1 cup frozen corn, thawed

1 medium tomato, diced

¼ cup diced red onion

1 jalapeño pepper, seeded and diced

¼ cup diced green pepper

¼ cup lime juice

¼ cup finely chopped fresh cilantro

1 teaspoon coarse salt

¼ teaspoon freshly ground black pepper

FOR CILANTRO-LIME RICE

Bring water to a boil in a medium-sized saucepan. Add rice and ½ teaspoon salt, then return to a boil. Reduce heat to medium. Simmer uncovered for 12 minutes, until water is absorbed and rice is tender. Then stir in lime juice and cilantro, and add up to an additional ½ teaspoon salt, to taste.

FOR AVOCADO CREMA

Place all ingredients in a food processor, and blend until smooth. Then set aside.

TO SERVE

Evenly divide rice on 4 to 6 plates. Unwrap Tamales and place on top of rice. Top with Corn Salsa and Avocado Crema.

CILANTRO-LIME RICE

1½ cups water

1 cup basmati rice

1 teaspoon coarse salt, divided

2 tablespoons lime juice

¼ cup finely chopped fresh cilantro

AVOCADO CREMA

1 avocado, diced

½ cup sour cream

¼ cup finely chopped fresh cilantro

1 teaspoon salt

2 tablespoons lime juice

PASTELÓN (MEAT PIE)

MAINS & SIDES

Dishes at Feast of the Three Kings pay tribute to Día de los Reyes Mago, a holiday celebrated in Spain, Latin America, and the Caribbean. This meat pie starts with sofrito, a base for many traditional dishes (refrigerate or freeze any leftover sofrito for other dishes).

SERVES 4

INTRODUCED 2018 • FEAST OF THE THREE KINGS HOLIDAY KITCHEN

FOR GREEN SOFRITO

Combine all ingredients in blender and purée until smooth. Set aside.

FOR SOFRITO GROUND BEEF

1. Heat canola oil in a large pan over medium heat. Add onions and sauté until translucent.

2. Add ground beef, stirring to break up beef. Add ¾ cup Green Sofrito, salt, pepper, and cumin; continue to stir until beef is fully cooked.

3. Add diced tomato, tomato paste, and Tabasco® sauce. Lower heat to medium-low and cook for an additional 5 to 8 minutes.

4. Stir in green olives. Consistency should be semiwet but not swimming in liquid. Set aside.

GREEN SOFRITO

10 large cloves garlic

¼ cup finely chopped fresh cilantro (remove large stems)

¼ cup finely chopped fresh culantro (remove large stems)

2 tablespoons chopped green onion

¼ cup chopped cubanelle pepper

½ cup chopped white onion

1 cup chopped green pepper

1 cup chopped red pepper

1 teaspoon dried oregano

⅛ teaspoon freshly ground black pepper

SOFRITO GROUND BEEF

1 tablespoon canola oil

3 tablespoons diced white onion

1 pound ground beef

¾ cup Green Sofrito

¼ teaspoon coarse salt

¼ teaspoon freshly ground black pepper

¼ teaspoon ground cumin

½ cup drained diced tomato

2 tablespoons tomato paste

¼ teaspoon Tabasco® sauce

FOR SWEET PLANTAIN MASH

1. Preheat oven 325°F. Place sweet plantains in a single layer on a parchment paper–lined baking sheet. Bake for 15 to 20 minutes until the plantains are slightly caramelized but not too dark.

2. Mash plantains and salt in a medium-sized mixing bowl. Slowly add chicken stock, mashing to a creamy mashed potatoes–style consistency—some lumps are okay. (Note: Depending on the plantains, you may not need all the stock.)

FOR PASTELÓN (MEAT PIE)

Preheat oven to 350°F. Spray a 2-quart baking dish with cooking spray, and then place in the Sofrito Ground Beef. Cover beef with Sweet Plantain Mash, and top with mozzarella cheese. Bake for 15 to 20 minutes, until meat pie is bubbly and cheese is golden brown.

3 tablespoons sliced Spanish green olives

SWEET PLANTAIN MASH

1 pound frozen sweet plantains, thawed (or 2 fresh plantains, peeled and sliced lengthwise)

½ teaspoon coarse salt

1 cup chicken stock

TOPPING

1 cup mozzarella cheese

BEEF BOURGUIGNON

MAINS & SIDES

One of the most popular dishes with festivalgoers, this hearty classic has it all: fork-tender beef brisket with bacon-infused wine sauce over crushed buttery red potatoes with a splash of sherry vinegar. And it's even better the next day.

SERVES 6

INTRODUCED 2020 · YUKON HOLIDAY KITCHEN

BEEF BOURGUIGNON

1 tablespoon unsalted butter

6 ounces smoked bacon, diced

3 pounds beef brisket or stew meat, trimmed and cut into 2-inch pieces

Coarse salt and freshly ground black pepper, to taste

4 cloves garlic, minced

1 large white onion, diced

1 large carrot, peeled and cut into ½-inch slices

1 pound cremini mushrooms, quartered

1 tablespoon fresh chopped rosemary

1 tablespoon fresh chopped thyme

2 tablespoons tomato paste

2 tablespoons flour

3 cups red wine (merlot, pinot noir, or chianti)

2 cups beef broth

½ cup sherry vinegar

12 small fresh or frozen pearl onions, peeled

2 tablespoons fresh chopped parsley, divided

FOR BEEF BOURGUIGNON

1 Heat butter and bacon in a large Dutch oven over medium heat and cook until bacon is brown and beginning to crisp. Remove bacon with a slotted spoon and set aside.

2 Pat beef dry and season generously with salt and pepper. Sear in Dutch oven with butter and bacon fat, 1 to 2 minutes per side, until browned. Remove from pan with slotted spoon and set aside.

3 Add garlic, onions, carrot, and mushrooms and sauté 6 minutes, until vegetables begin to soften. Stir in rosemary and thyme.

4 Add tomato paste and cook, stirring often, for 3 minutes, until paste begins to caramelize but does not burn.

5 Return beef and bacon to pan. Add flour and stir constantly for 5 minutes. Add wine, beef broth, and vinegar and stir to deglaze pot. Add pearl onions and bring to a boil over high heat. Reduce to a simmer and cook, covered, stirring occasionally, for 1½ hours until meat is tender and sauce is thickened. Add 1½ tablespoons of parsley and season with salt and pepper, to taste. Keep warm until ready to serve.

FOR SMASHED RED POTATOES

1 Bring a large stockpot of water to a boil. Add 1 tablespoon salt and the potatoes and boil for 10 to 15 minutes, until soft. Drain potatoes.

2 Return potatoes to pot and mash with a hand masher or electric mixer until just broken. Add butter, sour cream, and vinegar. Mix until potatoes are mashed but still lumpy.

3 Season with additional salt and white pepper, to taste.

TO SERVE

Divide Smashed Red Potatoes among 6 bowls. Ladle on Beef Bourguignon, and top with remaining chopped parsley.

SMASHED RED POTATOES

1 tablespoon coarse salt, plus more to taste

3 pounds red-skinned potatoes, washed

½ cup sour cream

½ cup unsalted butter, softened

2 tablespoons sherry vinegar

White pepper, to taste

WARM TURKEY SANDWICH

Sure, you can make this with Thanksgiving leftovers, but it's delicious when you're craving a taste of the holidays any time of year.

SERVES 4

INTRODUCED 2016 • AMERICAN HOLIDAY TABLE HOLIDAY KITCHEN

FOR TURKEY BREAST

Preheat oven to 350°F. Season turkey with salt and pepper. Place on a roasting pan. Cook for 1½ to 2 hours, until turkey reaches an internal temperature of 165°F. Let rest for 15 minutes, then carve 4 large pieces. Set aside.

FOR STUFFING BREAD

1. Preheat oven to 350°F. Spray a 9 × 13-inch baking sheet with nonstick cooking spray.

2. Heat butter in a medium-sized skillet over medium heat until melted. Add onions and celery and sauté for 8 minutes, until soft. Add fresh herbs, and stir to combine.

3. Combine dry stuffing mix with chicken broth in a large bowl. Add onions and celery mix. Season with salt and pepper, as needed.

4. Stir in eggs until combined. Spread stuffing in prepared 9 × 13-inch pan. Bake for 15 minutes. Cool for 30 minutes. Refrigerate for at least 2 hours.

FOR GREEN BEAN CASSEROLE

Preheat oven to 350°F. Spray an 8-inch square pan with nonstick cooking spray. Then trim stems from green beans. Place green beans, cream of mushroom soup, and milk in a medium-sized bowl. Stir to combine. When ready, pour into prepared 8-inch pan and bake for 25 minutes. Top with crispy onions and bake for 3 minutes. Keep warm until ready to serve.

TURKEY BREAST

1 (4- to 6-pound) turkey breast

2 tablespoons coarse salt

1 teaspoon freshly ground black pepper

STUFFING BREAD

¼ cup unsalted butter

1 cup diced white onion

¼ cup diced celery

1 tablespoon chopped fresh parsley

1 tablespoon chopped fresh thyme

1 tablespoon chopped fresh rosemary

1 tablespoon chopped fresh sage

1 (6-ounce) box dry stuffing mix

1 cup turkey or chicken broth, hot

Coarse salt and freshly ground black pepper, to taste

2 eggs, lightly beaten

GREEN BEAN CASSEROLE

1 pound fresh green beans

1 (10-ounce) can cream of mushroom soup

½ cup milk

2 cups crispy onions

FOR MASHED POTATOES

1 Place diced potatoes in a large saucepan. Cover potatoes with cold water and bring to a boil over high heat.

2 Reduce heat to simmer and cook for 10 minutes, until potatoes are soft. Drain water from potatoes. While potatoes are cooking, melt butter in a small saucepan over low heat. Add milk and stir to combine. Keep warm.

3 Place potatoes in a bowl with half of the warm butter-and-milk mixture. Mash using an electric mixer, adding additional butter and milk until desired consistency is reached.

4 Season with salt, white pepper, and nutmeg. Keep warm until ready to serve.

MASHED POTATOES

4 russet potatoes, peeled and diced

¼ cup unsalted butter

½ cup milk

Coarse salt, to taste

½ teaspoon white pepper

½ teaspoon nutmeg

RIGHT: A holiday window display at the Germany pavilion in World Showcase at EPCOT, 2021.

(RECIPE CONTINUES ON PAGE 188)

WARM TURKEY SANDWICH

(CONTINUED)

FOR TURKEY GRAVY

1. Melt the butter in a medium-sized saucepan. Add flour and cook, whisking constantly until golden brown and smooth.

2. Whisk in turkey stock and heavy cream. Bring to a boil over medium-high heat. Reduce heat to medium-low and cook 5 minutes, until thick. Stir in white pepper, thyme, and sage. Keep warm until ready to serve.

TO SERVE

1. Preheat broiler to high. Cut stuffing into 8 pieces and place on a baking sheet. Broil for 1 minute on each side, until toasted.

2. Place 1 piece of Stuffing Bread on each plate. Top each piece of bread with a quarter of the Mashed Potatoes and a slice of Turkey Breast. Cover with remaining 4 slices of Stuffing Bread.

3. Ladle gravy on top of the sandwich. Top each sandwich with cranberry sauce. Serve with Green Bean Casserole on the side.

TURKEY GRAVY

1 tablespoon unsalted butter

2 tablespoons flour

2 cups turkey or chicken stock

1½ tablespoons heavy cream

Coarse salt, to taste

½ teaspoon white pepper

½ tablespoon chopped fresh thyme

½ tablespoon chopped fresh sage

TOPPING

½ cup canned cranberry sauce

OPPOSITE: The main holiday tree and Spaceship Earth are reflected in the waters around World Celebration during the 2021 EPCOT International Festival of the Holidays.

CLASSIC POTATO LATKES

MAINS & SIDES

A plant-based version of the traditional Jewish potato pancake from the L'Chaim Holiday Kitchen is a fan favorite at EPCOT Festival of the Holidays.

MAKES 10-12

INTRODUCED 2019 • L'CHAIM HOLIDAY KITCHEN

POTATO LATKES

4 medium Yukon Gold potatoes

½ large onion

Oil, for frying

½ cup matzo meal

1 large egg, beaten

1 teaspoon coarse salt

½ teaspoon ground white pepper

FOR POTATO LATKES

1. Cut potatoes into large chunks and shred using a food processor fitted with a shredding disk. Immediately place potatoes in cold water to prevent browning.

2. Shred onion using food processor to same size as potato shreds.

3. Drain potato shreds. Place drained shredded potatoes and onions in the center of a clean tea towel. Wrap shreds in cloth and twist to remove excess liquid.

4. Pour potatoes and onions into a clean, dry bowl. Stir with a fork to evenly mix.

5. With caution, heat 1 inch of oil in a large skillet over medium heat until it reaches 325°F. While oil is heating, stir matzo meal, egg, salt, and white pepper into potatoes and onions, using a fork.

6. Scoop ¼ cup of the latke mix and form into a disk. Carefully place in oil using a large slotted spatula, and cook for 2 to 3 minutes per side, being careful not to break latke while turning. Drain on paper towels.

FOR HOT SMOKED SALMON SALAD

Chop whites of hardboiled eggs and discard yolks. Combine egg whites, warmed salmon, red onions, and capers in a medium-sized bowl. Keep warm until ready to serve.

FOR DILL SOUR CREAM

Combine sour cream and dill in a small bowl. Season with salt and pepper, to taste. Refrigerate until ready to serve.

TO SERVE

Top each Potato Latke with Hot Smoked Salmon Salad, Dill Sour Cream, and fresh micro chervil.

OPPOSITE: Guests enjoy a treat from L'Chaim Holiday Kitchen during the 2021 EPCOT International Festival of the Holidays.

HOT SMOKED SALMON SALAD

2 hardboiled eggs

½ pound flaked smoked salmon, warmed

¼ red onion, diced

2 tablespoons capers, chopped

DILL SOUR CREAM

1 cup sour cream

1 tablespoon chopped fresh dill

Coarse salt and freshly ground black pepper, to taste

TOPPING

Micro chervil

SWEET SPICED NOODLE KUGEL WITH LEMON CREAM AND CRANBERRIES

Kugel, a traditional Jewish casserole, can be sweet or savory—this thick, eggy version is the perfect amount of sweet with a hint of cinnamon. You can make it the day before, store it in the fridge, and reheat (or it's delicious at room temperature).

MAKES 1 (9 × 13-INCH) PAN

INTRODUCED 2016 • NOSH & NIBBLES FESTIVAL MARKETPLACE

FOR KUGEL

1 Preheat oven to 350°F. Grease a 9 × 13-inch baking pan with butter. Set aside. Bring a large pot of water to a boil. Add egg noodles and boil for 4 to 5 minutes, until al dente. Drain and set aside.

2 Whisk eggs and sugar in a large bowl until smooth. Add cottage cheese, sour cream, and melted butter, whisking until combined. Then add cinnamon, allspice, salt, and cranberries to egg mixture. Stir in noodles.

3 Pour into prepared baking pan, making sure to press noodles down and smooth the top. Bake for 50 to 60 minutes, until top is golden and filling is set.

FOR LEMON CREAM AND TO SERVE

Combine sour cream, lemon zest, and sugar in a small bowl. Stir until blended. Refrigerate until ready to use. When ready to serve, cut warm Kugel to desired size. Top with drizzle of Lemon Cream and sprinkle with sugar-frosted corn flake cereal and dried cranberries.

KUGEL

1 pound wide egg noodles

7 eggs

½ cup sugar

1 (16-ounce) container cottage cheese

1 (16-ounce) container sour cream

½ cup unsalted butter, melted and cooled

1½ teaspoons cinnamon

⅛ teaspoon ground allspice

¼ teaspoon salt

1 cup dried cranberries

LEMON CREAM

1 cup sour cream

Zest of 2 lemons

1 tablespoon sugar

TOPPINGS

1 cup sugar-frosted corn flake cereal

1 cup dried cranberries

ABOVE, BOTTOM: The nighttime spectacular shows of Paradise Bay at Disney California Adventure, such as the dancing waters shown here in 2015, add to the magic of an evening at Disney Festival of Holidays.

BOK CHOY AND MUSHROOM DUMPLINGS

Finely chop the vegetables and taste the filling for seasoning—don't skimp on the black pepper. For a quick sauce, mix equal parts wine vinegar and soy sauce with a dash of sesame oil.

MAKES 40 DUMPLINGS

INTRODUCED 2023 • WRAPPED IN LOVE FESTIVAL MARKETPLACE

FOR BLACK GARLIC SAUCE

Use a fine grater to grate garlic into a paste. Whisk garlic paste with remaining ingredients in a large bowl. Refrigerate and use as dipping sauce or pour over dumplings.

FOR BOK CHOY AND MUSHROOM DUMPLINGS

1. Heat sesame oil in a large skillet over medium heat. Add shiitake mushrooms, carrots, and onions and sauté for 10 minutes. Stir in bok choy, sugar, salt, and pepper and cook until bok choy is tender, about 3 minutes. Remove from heat and cool.

2. Fill center of wonton wrapper with 1 scant tablespoon filling. Repeat until all filling is used. Fold diagonally in half, sealing edges with egg wash. Place on parchment-lined baking sheet. Repeat with remaining filling and wrappers.

3. Place in bamboo steamer lined with cabbage leaves or parchment paper over a pot of boiling water, leaving space between dumplings. Cover tightly and steam until filling is firm and cooked through, 8 to 10 minutes. Repeat with remaining dumplings. Serve hot with Black Garlic Dipping Sauce.

BLACK GARLIC DIPPING SAUCE

1 clove black garlic

1 cup low-sodium soy sauce

1 cup rice vinegar

½ cup black vinegar

1 tablespoon agave

½ tablespoon sambal

1 tablespoon sliced green onion

BOK CHOY AND MUSHROOM DUMPLINGS

1 tablespoon sesame oil

½ pound shiitake mushrooms, finely chopped

1 cup shredded carrot

1½ cups finely chopped onions

½ pound bok choy, small dice

2 teaspoons sugar

2 teaspoons salt

1 teaspoon coarsely ground black pepper

40 wonton wrappers

1 egg, beaten

OPPOSITE, BOTTOM: Mushu greets a young guest during the 2022 Lunar New Year Celebration at Disney California Adventure.

DANCING FIRECRACKER

The spicy honey gives a kick to this nonalcoholic beverage, full of fruity flavor from pineapple and guava. The Spicy Honey Syrup is guaranteed to make you dance.

SERVES 1

INTRODUCED 2023 • RED DRAGON SPICE TRADERS FESTIVAL MARKETPLACE

SPICY HONEY SYRUP

¼ cup hot honey

¼ cup hot water

DANCING FIRECRACKER

4½ ounces guava nectar

3¼ ounces pineapple juice

1 ounce lime juice

1½ ounces hibiscus syrup

¾ ounce Spicy Honey Syrup

Lime wheel, for garnish

FOR SPICY HONEY SYRUP

Stir together in a small saucepan over medium heat until well combined. Refrigerate until ready to use. (This will last indefinitely in refrigerator.)

FOR DANCING FIRECRACKER

1. Stir together guava nectar, hibiscus syrup, pineapple, and lime juice in a 16-ounce glass.

2. Stir in honey syrup. Fill with ice and garnish with lime wheel.

GUAVA-MELON LASSI

MOCKTAILS & COCKTAILS

Drink your dessert with this light, creamy yogurt drink starring guava with a backbeat of melon and a finish of cinnamon whipped cream. You can make your own cantaloupe syrup by combining ½ cup sugar and ½ cup water in a small saucepan and cooking over medium heat, stirring occasionally until sugar is melted. Stir in 1 cup puréed cantaloupe. Refrigerate for up to two days.

SERVES 4

INTRODUCED 2022 • A TWIST ON TRADITION FESTIVAL MARKETPLACE

CINNAMON WHIPPED CREAM

¾ cup heavy whipping cream

2 tablespoons cinnamon syrup

GUAVA-MELON LASSI

1½ cups guava nectar

½ cup nonfat yogurt

⅓ cup water

½ cup cantaloupe syrup

2 tablespoon honey

1 cup ice

TOPPING

Honey-flavored cereal

FOR CINNAMON WHIPPED CREAM

Combine heavy whipping cream and cinnamon syrup in the bowl of an electric mixer fitted with a whisk attachment. Whip until medium peaks form. Place in a piping bag and refrigerate until ready to serve.

FOR GUAVA-MELON LASSI

Combine guava nectar, nonfat yogurt, water, cantaloupe syrup, and honey in a large pitcher and stir until combined. Fill rocks glasses with ice, and pour mixture over ice. Top with Cinnamon Whipped Cream and honey-flavored cereal.

CHURRO-TOFFEE COLD BREW LATTE

All the flavor of a churro with a kick of caffeine—the churro syrup keeps for up to a week in the refrigerator.

SERVES 1

INTRODUCED 2022 • FAVORITE THINGS FESTIVAL MARKETPLACE

FOR CHURRO-TOFFEE SYRUP

Combine demerara sugar, cinnamon sugar, water, salt, and vanilla bean paste in a medium-sized saucepan. Cook over medium heat, stirring occasionally, until sugar is melted. Cool to room temperature before serving. Leftover syrup can be stored in an airtight container for up to one week.

FOR ALMOND MILK CHURRO FOAM

Combine almond milk and Churro-Toffee Syrup in a milk frother or blender and blend until frothy.

FOR CHURRO-TOFFEE COLD BREW LATTE

Add cold brew coffee, unsweetened almond milk, and house-made Churro-Toffee Syrup together and mix thoroughly in a cocktail shaker. Add ice to a tall cup and pour in cold brew. Then top with Almond Milk Churro Foam and sprinkle toffee pieces on top.

CHURRO-TOFFEE SYRUP

⅓ cup demerara sugar

⅓ cup cinnamon sugar

⅓ cup water

1 teaspoon salt

1 teaspoon vanilla bean paste (or vanilla extract)

ALMOND MILK CHURRO FOAM

¼ cup unsweetened almond milk

1½ teaspoons Churro-Toffee Syrup

CHURRO-TOFFEE COLD BREW LATTE

1 cup cold brew coffee

3 tablespoons Churro-Toffee Syrup

2 tablespoons unsweetened almond milk

½ cup ice cubes

¼ cup Almond Milk Churro Foam

1 tablespoon toffee pieces

HORCHATA

Icy cold, sweet and rich with a base of soaked rice, this traditional Mexican drink is a treat any time of year.

SERVES 1-2

INTRODUCED 2017 • ¡VIVA NAVIDAD! FESTIVAL MARKETPLACE

RICE BASE

2 cinnamon sticks

1 cup jasmine rice

2 cups filtered water

HORCHATA

¾ cup whole milk

¾ cup condensed milk

¾ teaspoon vanilla syrup

1 cup ice

TOPPINGS

Whipped cream

Sprinkles

Colored Sugar

ABOVE: Chip 'n' Dale hug guests on Buena Vista Street at Disney California Adventure during the 2012 Disney Festival of Holidays.

FOR RICE BASE

Combine cinnamon sticks, jasmine rice, and water in container and cover with lid. Allow to sit in refrigerator overnight or for a minimum of 8 hours to ensure cinnamon sticks and rice are softened. Blend and strain through cheesecloth. Then set aside.

FOR HORCHATA

Combine whole milk and condensed milk in a large container, and stir in Rice Base. Stir in vanilla syrup. Then add ice to serving cup, and pour Horchata over ice. Top with whipped cream, sprinkles, and colored sugar.

MISTLETOE MULE

You don't have to snuggle under the mistletoe to enjoy this refreshing drink! A twist on a classic mule with cranberry juice and agave syrup garnished with a sprig of rosemary and a cranberry.

SERVES 1

INTRODUCED 2022 • SONOMA TERRACE FESTIVAL MARKETPLACE

2 ounces vodka

2 ounces cranberry juice

½ ounce lime juice

½ ounce agave syrup

3 ounces ginger beer

1 fresh rosemary sprig

3 cranberries, fresh or frozen

Add vodka, cranberry juice, lime juice, agave syrup, and ginger beer into a copper mug. Stir gently and fill with ice. Garnish with a rosemary sprig and cranberries.

VANILLA PEAR MULE

Pear and ginger is a lovely combination in this crisp cocktail.

SERVES 1

INTRODUCED 2019 • A TWIST ON TRADITION FESTIVAL MARKETPLACE

1¼ ounces vodka

4 ounces pear nectar

1 ounce vanilla syrup

1 cup ice, divided

2 ounces ginger beer

1 edible orchid, for serving

Combine vodka, pear nectar, and vanilla syrup in cocktail shaker with ice. Shake well and strain into 16-ounce copper mule mug over fresh ice. Fill with ginger beer, and top with edible orchid.

SWEET POTATO PIES

Perfect for a party, these mini-pies are layers of deliciousness with a crunchy streusel topping, spiced whipped cream, and candied pecans.

MAKES 6 SMALL PIES

INTRODUCED 2016 • SOUTHERN HOME HOLIDAYS FESTIVAL MARKETPLACE

FOR CANDIED PECANS

1. Preheat oven to 325°F. Line baking sheet with parchment paper or silicone baking mat.

2. Combine water and sugar in a small saucepan and bring to boil. Add pecans and remove from heat. Stir pecans and leave in syrup for 15 minutes.

3. Strain water from pecans and place pecans on prepared baking sheet. Bake for 3 to 6 minutes, until pecans are shiny.

FOR SWEET POTATO FILLING

1. Preheat oven to 350°F. Poke holes in bottom of each thawed pie crust with a fork. Bake for 8 minutes and set aside to cool.

2. Drain sweet potatoes and place in electric mixer. Mix on medium speed until very smooth. Add sugar, salt, vanilla extract, and nutmeg. Mix until combined. Add eggs, one at a time, mixing until fully incorporated. Slowly add melted butter until combined.

3. Pour sweet potato filling into cooled pie crusts and smooth filling. Set aside.

CANDIED PECANS

½ cup water

½ cup sugar

½ cup pecan halves

SWEET POTATO FILLING

6 (4-inch) frozen pie crusts, thawed

1 (15-ounce) can sweet potatoes

½ cup sugar

1 teaspoon salt

2 teaspoons vanilla extract

¼ teaspoon ground nutmeg

2 eggs

2 tablespoons unsalted butter, melted

FOR PECAN STREUSEL

1   Combine brown sugar, sugar, all-purpose flour, bread flour, cinnamon, and salt in electric mixer. Add softened butter. Mix until crumbly.

2   Add vanilla extract and pecans and mix on low speed. Add melted butter and mix until moist. Set aside.

FOR SPICED WHIPPED CREAM

1   Sift powdered sugar and cinnamon into small bowl. Set aside.

2   Place heavy cream in the bowl of an electric mixer fitted with whisk attachment. Whisk on low speed for one minute and then increase to high speed. Beat until soft peaks form.

3   Slowly add cinnamon and powdered sugar and beat to medium peaks. Refrigerate until ready to serve.

FOR SWEET POTATO PIES

1   Preheat oven to 350°F. Sprinkle ½ cup Pecan Streusel on top of each pie and bake for 18 minutes.

2   Cool to room temperature and dust with powdered sugar. Place one dollop of Spiced Whipped Cream and one Candied Pecan on top of each pie.

PECAN STREUSEL

1½ cups light brown sugar

½ cup sugar

½ cup all-purpose flour

¾ cup bread flour

1 tablespoon ground cinnamon

¼ teaspoon salt

¾ cup unsalted butter, softened

¾ cup chopped pecans

¼ cup unsalted butter, melted

SPICED WHIPPED CREAM

2 tablespoons powdered sugar

½ teaspoon ground cinnamon

1 cup heavy cream

TOPPING

Powdered sugar

ALMOND-SPICED CAKE WITH GINGER MOUSSE, ORANGE GANACHE, AND SESAME TUILE

It's a taste of Morocco with almond as the dominant flavor, topped with airy ginger mousse and a subtle bright kick from the orange ganache. Edible food color spray can be found online or at any craft store.

SERVES 12

INTRODUCED 2021 • TANGERINE CAFÉ HOLIDAY KITCHEN

FOR GINGER MOUSSE

1. Combine water and gelatin in a small microwave-safe bowl; set aside. Heat milk, ginger, and sugar in a small saucepan over medium heat until milk begins to simmer. Reduce heat to medium-low.

2. Place egg yolks in a small bowl and whisk. Slowly add half of the hot milk mixture and continue whisking. Pour into saucepan with remaining milk mixture.

3. Cook, stirring constantly, until custard begins to bubble and thicken. Remove from heat and strain custard into a medium-sized bowl.

4. Place gelatin-water mixture in microwave for 30 seconds. Stir to dissolve gelatin. Add to custard and stir to combine. Cool at room temperature for 30 minutes. Cover and refrigerate 4 hours, until custard is fully set.

5. Whip heavy cream in the bowl of an electric mixer fitted with a whisk attachment until medium peaks form. Fold into cooled custard.

GINGER MOUSSE

½ cup water

1 (¼-ounce) packet unflavored gelatin

2½ cups whole milk

2 teaspoons ground ginger

¼ cup sugar

4 egg yolks

1 cup heavy whipping cream

ALMOND-SPICED CAKE

1 cup all-purpose flour

2 teaspoons baking powder

½ teaspoon salt

½ teaspoon ground cinnamon

¼ teaspoon ground cloves

¼ teaspoon ground nutmeg

½ teaspoon ground ginger

¾ cup almond paste

1 cup unsalted butter, room temperature

1⅓ cups sugar

4 eggs

1 teaspoon vanilla extract

1 teaspoon almond extract

Orange edible food color spray, optional for serving

FOR ALMOND-SPICED CAKE

1 Preheat oven to 350°F. Grease a 9 × 13-inch baking pan with nonstick cooking spray and set aside. Sift flour, baking powder, salt, cinnamon, cloves, nutmeg, and ginger into a large bowl; set aside.

2 In the bowl of an electric mixer fitted with a paddle attachment, cream almond paste and butter until smooth. Add sugar and beat on medium speed until fluffy.

3 Reduce mixer speed to low and add eggs, one at a time. Add vanilla extract and almond extract and combine on low speed until incorporated.

4 Slowly add reserved flour mixture and beat on medium speed until smooth.

5 Spread into prepared pan and bake 15 minutes, until a toothpick inserted in the center comes out clean. Cool completely.

6 Spread Ginger Mousse over cake. Tightly cover pan with foil. Freeze for at least 4 hours or up to 24 hours.

FOR SESAME TUILE

1 Preheat oven to 325°F. Line 2 baking sheets with parchment paper; set aside.

2 Whisk powdered sugar, lemon juice, and orange juice in a medium-sized bowl. Add flour, sesame seeds, and melted butter and stir until smooth. Scoop teaspoon-sized balls of dough onto prepared baking sheets. Each baking sheet should have 9 balls of dough.

3 Bake for 8 minutes. If desired, use a small rolling pin to curve each tuile after cooling for 5 minutes. Cool completely before serving.

SESAME TUILE

½ cup powdered sugar

1½ teaspoons lemon juice

2 teaspoons orange juice

1½ tablespoons all-purpose flour

2 tablespoons white sesame seeds

2 tablespoons black sesame seeds

1½ tablespoons unsalted butter, melted

ABOVE, BOTTOM: A twilight view of the Morocco pavilion in World Showcase at EPCOT, 2014.

(RECIPE CONTINUES ON PAGE 206)

ALMOND-SPICED CAKE WITH GINGER MOUSSE, ORANGE GANACHE, AND SESAME TUILE

(CONTINUED)

FOR ORANGE GANACHE

1. Combine heavy cream, orange juice, and orange zest in a small saucepan. Bring to a boil over medium heat.

2. While heavy cream is heating, place milk chocolate and dark chocolate in a large bowl. Add boiling cream to chocolate and let rest for 1 minute. Whisk until smooth.

3. Place plastic wrap on top of the ganache and allow it to set up at room temperature for 30 minutes.

TO SERVE

1. Remove Almond-Spiced Cake from freezer, uncover, and evenly spray with the edible food color spray. (If preferred, this step may be omitted. It will not change the flavor profile.)

2. Carefully heat your cake-slicing knife by dipping it in a tall container of very hot water or holding it under hot running water for a few seconds. Wipe it dry before cutting the cake to desired number of pieces, reheating the knife when needed.

3. Top each cake slice with Ginger Mousse. Then spread, or pipe, Orange Ganache on Ginger Mousse, and top with Sesame Tuile.

ORANGE GANACHE

½ cup heavy whipping cream

½ cup orange juice

1 teaspoon orange zest

1 cup chopped milk chocolate

1 cup chopped dark chocolate

SNOWBALL COOKIES

With just six ingredients and powdered sugar for finishing, these are a favorite on any holiday cookie tray.

MAKES 48

INTRODUCED 2021 • HOLIDAY HEARTH DESSERTS HOLIDAY KITCHEN

FOR SNOWBALL COOKIES

1. Preheat oven to 350°F. Line 2 baking sheets with parchment paper or silicone baking mats and set aside. Then place pecan halves, all-purpose flour, and salt in food processor. Pulse until pecans are finely ground.

2. In the bowl of an electric mixer fitted with a paddle attachment, cream butter and 1¼ cups powdered sugar until fluffy. Add vanilla and mix on medium speed until incorporated. Then add pecan and flour mixture and mix on low speed until fully mixed.

3. Use a 1-inch cookie scoop to shape cookies into smooth balls. Place remaining ¾ cup powdered sugar in a small bowl.

4. Roll cookies in powdered sugar and place 12 cookies on each prepared baking sheet. Bake for 14 to 16 minutes, until golden brown. Then cool for 5 minutes.

TO SERVE

Place powdered sugar in a sifter. Dust warm cookies with powdered sugar. Then cool to room temperature before serving.

SNOWBALL COOKIES

3 cups pecan halves

2¾ cups all-purpose flour

¼ teaspoon salt

1 cup unsalted butter, softened

2 cups powdered sugar, divided

1½ teaspoons vanilla extract

TOPPING

½ cup powdered sugar

STOLLEN

Stollen has been a Christmas classic in Germany for centuries (some historians date its origin back to 1329!) and is one of the most beloved of all holiday pastries. Sweet and flaky and studded with candied fruit, the yeast bread is even better a few days after it's baked. Pair with glogg, the perfect winter drink made with red wine, warm spices, and a shot of a distilled spirit like rum or vodka.

MAKES 1 LARGE LOAF

INTRODUCED 2014 • CHRISTKINDLMARKT HOLIDAY KITCHEN

SOAKER

1 cup mixed candied fruit, preferably orange and lemon peel

½ cup sliced almonds

1 cup golden raisins

½ cup orange-flavored liqueur

VANILLA SUGAR

1 cup powdered sugar

1 cup sugar

1 vanilla bean

STARTER SPONGE

1 tablespoon active dry yeast

1 cup warm milk (110°F)

1½ cups bread flour

2 cups all-purpose flour

FOR SOAKER

Combine fruit, almonds, and golden raisins. Pour liqueur over fruit and nuts, mixing well. Cover and marinate at room temperature for 3 days, shaking or stirring occasionally.

FOR VANILLA SUGAR

Mix together sugars in a small bowl. Cut vanilla bean in half, scrape out seeds, and add seeds to sugar mixture. Mix well, and then add the scraped pod to the sugar mixture. Cover tightly, and set aside for 3 days.

FOR STARTER SPONGE

1 Pour yeast into milk and stir. Let sit for 10 minutes. Place bread flour in the bowl of an electric mixer fitted with a dough hook attachment.

2 Slowly pour milk-yeast mixture into the bowl, and mix on low speed for 2 minutes. Turn to medium-high speed for 3 to 4 minutes or until starter sponge is smooth. Turn mixer off.

3 Cover starter sponge with all-purpose flour, allowing flour to rest over sponge. Do not turn mixer on or move; let sponge proof until you see cracks or crevices forming through the flour, about 8 to 10 minutes. (This indicates the dough is alive and the yeast is activated.)

FOR DOUGH

1 Place almond paste in a small bowl. Make a well in center of almond paste. Put vanilla bean paste in center of well. Place sugar, salt, lemon zest, and almond-vanilla bean paste on top of Starter Sponge in mixing bowl. Mix for 30 seconds.

2 Add egg and butter; continue mixing for another 1½ minutes. Turn to medium-high and mix for 3 more minutes. Turn mixer to low speed for 1 minute and add Soaker, 1 cup at a time, mixing well after each addition.

DOUGH

¼ cup almond paste

1 teaspoon vanilla bean paste (or vanilla extract)

¼ cup sugar

Pinch salt

1 tablespoon finely grated lemon zest

Starter Sponge

1 large egg

½ cup unsalted butter, softened

Soaker

Butter Glaze (see recipe on page 210)

(RECIPE CONTINUES ON PAGE 210)

STOLLEN

FOR DOUGH (CONTINUED)

3 Turn dough out onto floured board. Knead into a ball, making sure top is smooth; roll into a log, making sure there are no seams on the ends. (There will be a slight seam on bottom.) Cover with plastic wrap and allow to rise for 5 minutes until not quite doubled in size.

4 With a ½-inch dowel rod, begin rolling the log, starting from the center. Roll forward, then backward, until there are two humps separated by about 5 inches of dough where dowel rod rolled and thinned the dough. Fold top (closest) hump over the thinned middle to meet the edge of the bottom hump.

5 Let loaf rise on top of oven or other warm area for 10 to 15 minutes. Preheat oven to 375°F. Bake loaf for 1 minutes at 375°F, then reduce temperature to 325°F and continue to bake for 40 to 45 minutes or until bread is dark golden.

6 Remove from oven and remove any burned fruit from top. Poke 12 to 15 holes in bread with a skewer. Brush with Butter Glaze on top, sides, and bottom.

FOR BUTTER GLAZE

While stollen is baking, add powdered sugar and vanilla bean paste to melted butter in a saucepan over low heat. Keep warm to brush over warm bread.

TO SERVE

Roll warm bread covered in Butter Glaze in Vanilla Sugar. Cool and cut into ½-inch slices to serve.

BUTTER GLAZE

1 cup unsalted butter, melted

¼ cup powdered sugar

1 teaspoon vanilla bean paste (or vanilla extract)

ABOVE: The ornate statue of Saint George in the center of the Germany pavilion in World Showcase at EPCOT, 2021.

MAPLE PECAN BARK

The hardest part of making this bark—a cross between toffee and brittle—is getting it to the right temperature so that it properly sets. You can find maple extract and maple sugar online or in specialty stores.

MAKES 24 PIECES

INTRODUCED 2016 • CANADA POPCORN CART HOLIDAY KITCHEN

¾ cup pecans

1 teaspoon sea salt

1 cup unsalted butter

1 cup sugar

¼ cup water

1½ cups semisweet chocolate chips, divided

1½ tablespoons maple sugar

1 Combine pecans and sea salt in a medium-sized pan. Toast over medium heat, stirring constantly for 1 to 2 minutes, until brown and fragrant. Chop into small pieces and set aside.

2 Melt butter in a medium-sized saucepan over medium-low heat. Once butter is melted, add sugar and water, stirring continuously until temperature reaches 295°F. Immediately pour onto baking sheet lined with a silicone baking mat and spread into a 9 × 13-inch rectangle. Cool for at least 3 hours.

3 Melt ¾ cup chocolate chips in a small bowl and spread over one side of the cooled bark. Immediately sprinkle half of the chopped pecans and maple sugar over the chocolate. Then cool for 2 hours, until chocolate is set.

4 Melt remaining ¾ cup chocolate chips. Turn bark over and spread chocolate on the other half of the bark. Sprinkle with remaining chopped pecans and maple sugar. Cool for 2 hours, until chocolate is set. To serve, break into 24 pieces. Store in an airtight container for up to 7 days.

CHOCOLATE CRINKLE COOKIES

These rich, fudgy chocolate cookies are coated with powdered sugar that cracks—or crinkles—when they bake, giving them a snow-capped, wintry look. Note that the dough needs to refrigerate for at least 3 hours (up to 24 hours) prior to baking. For a plant-based version of these delicious cookies, in place of eggs, mix 2 tablespoons ground flaxseed and 5 tablespoons water in a small bowl or cup. Let sit for 5 minutes to thicken.

1 cup all-purpose flour

½ cup unsweetened cocoa powder

1 teaspoon baking powder

¼ teaspoon salt

¾ cup sugar

¼ cup vegetable oil

2 large eggs

1 teaspoon vanilla extract

½ cup powdered sugar (for coating the cookies)

MAKES 12-14

INTRODUCED 2019 • FEAST OF THE THREE KINGS HOLIDAY KITCHEN

1 Whisk flour, cocoa powder, baking powder, and salt in a medium-sized bowl until combined; set aside. Add sugar and vegetable oil in the bowl of a stand mixer. Beat on medium-low until combined. Add eggs and vanilla extract, beating on medium-high until combined. Gradually add flour mixture, beating on medium-low speed until combined. (Note: The consistency will be similar to a brownie batter but will firm up with chilling.)

2 Tightly seal bowl with plastic wrap and refrigerate for at least 3 hours (or up to 24 hours) until dough is completely chilled through and able to be rolled into balls.

3 After dough is completely chilled and ready to be baked, preheat oven to 350°F. Line large cookie sheet with parchment paper.

ABOVE: Guests at the Norway pavilion in World Showcase during the 2021 EPCOT International Festival of the Holidays.

4 Fill small bowl with powdered sugar; set aside. Remove and unwrap dough. Using medium-sized cookie scoop to measure out dough, roll into round balls. Roll dough ball in powdered sugar until completely covered on all sides.

5 Place cookie balls at least 2 inches apart on prepared baking sheet. Bake for 8 to 10 minutes; do not overbake. Allow cookies to cool on baking sheet for 3 minutes.

6 Transfer cookies to wire rack, and let them cool until they reach room temperature. Store in sealed container for up to 5 days or freeze for up to 3 months.

ALFAJORE (VANILLA SHORTBREAD COOKIES)

Popular in Latin America, this classic butter cookie is sandwiched with sweet dulce de leche filling and rolled in coconut—you can use store-bought dulce de leche to make the recipe easier. We think they're best when they're fresh!

MAKES 6-8

INTRODUCED 2022 • NOCHEBUENA COCINA HOLIDAY KITCHEN

FOR SHORTBREAD

1 Preheat oven to 325°F. Line baking sheet with parchment paper, and set aside. Then combine all-purpose flour and cornstarch in a small bowl; set aside.

2 Cream butter and powdered sugar in the bowl of an electric mixer fitted with a paddle attachment until fluffy. Add egg yolk and vanilla extract and mix on medium speed, scraping sides occasionally, until fully incorporated.

3 Add reserved flour mixture and combine on low speed until dry dough starts to come together. Remove from bowl and knead on floured surface until dough is soft.

4 Roll dough to ½-inch thickness. Cut into 2½-inch circles. Place on prepared baking pan, leaving 2-inches between each cookie. Bake for 10 to 12 minutes, until lightly browned. Then cool on wire racks.

FOR ALFAJORE

Spoon dulce de leche into a piping bag. Place half of the Shortbread, bottom side up, on a flat surface. Pipe dulce de leche onto each cookie. Top with remaining cookies. Coat sides of cookies with shredded coconut and dust tops with powdered sugar.

SHORTBREAD

2 cups all-purpose flour

½ cup cornstarch

¾ cup unsalted butter, softened

½ cup powdered sugar

1 egg yolk

1 tablespoon vanilla extract

ALFAJORE

1 (14-ounce) can dulce de leche

12–16 cookies

½ cup shredded coconut

¼ cup powdered sugar

OPPOSITE, BOTTOM and ABOVE: Guests near the main holiday tree during the 2021 EPCOT International Festival of the Holidays.

LINZER BAR COOKIES

SWEET ENDINGS & DESSERTS

Linz is a city in Austria and home to the traditional European Christmas pastry known as a Linzer torte, a tart of rich buttery dough filled with preserves and topped with a lattice crust. These chewy bar cookies are a twist on the original.

MAKES 20

INTRODUCED 2014 • CHRISTKINDLMARKT HOLIDAY KITCHEN

½ cup unsalted butter, softened

½ cup sugar

2 eggs

1 cup all-purpose flour

¾ cup hazelnut flour

1 teaspoon ground cinnamon

½ teaspoon baking powder

1 cup raspberry jam

Powdered sugar, for serving

1. Line a 9-inch-square baking pan with foil, letting edges hang over sides. Butter foil; set pan aside.

2. Combine butter and sugar in a large bowl; beat with an electric mixer at medium-high speed until light and fluffy.

3. Add eggs one at a time, mixing well until combined. Then combine all-purpose flour, hazelnut flour, cinnamon, and baking powder in a medium-sized bowl, whisking to combine. Add to butter mixture. Mix at low speed until just combined.

4. Place 2 cups dough into prepared pan, spreading evenly. Spread raspberry jam on top of dough. Then place remaining dough in a heavy-duty piping bag, and cut a ½-inch hole in corner tip of bag.

5. Pipe strips of dough diagonally from corner to corner on top of the jam layer, leaving a 1½-inch space in between each line and making a lattice pattern. Refrigerate 20 minutes.

6. While dough chills, preheat oven to 350°F. Then bake approximately 35 minutes, until golden. Cool completely.

7. Use overhang of foil to lift Linzer out of pan; peel foil away and cut into 20 squares. Dust with powdered sugar before serving.

OPPOSITE, BOTTOM: Guests chat with Santa Claus during the 2022 EPCOT International Festival of the Holidays.

SPACESHIP EARTH COOKIES WITH SALTED CARAMEL GANACHE

These cookies take some time, but you can make the salted caramel ganache a day or two ahead. If you don't have a Spaceship Earth cookie cutter, you can just use a 3½-inch round, fluted cookie cutter.

MAKES 15–18

INTRODUCED 2020 • HOLIDAY HEARTH HOLIDAY KITCHEN

FOR SALTED CARAMEL CHOCOLATE GANACHE

1. Pour chocolate chips into medium-sized bowl and set aside.

2. Combine sugar, water, and lemon juice in a small saucepan over medium heat and stir until sugar is just dissolved. Bring syrup to a boil, without stirring, and allow to boil an additional 2 to 3 minutes, until syrup is a deep amber color and 350°F.

3. Remove from heat and stir in a third of the heavy cream. When cream stops bubbling, add an additional third of the cream, and finally the rest. Stir in butter, one piece at a time. Add salt.

4. Cook over medium heat, stirring constantly, for 2 to 3 minutes, until cream and butter are fully incorporated into caramel.

5. Pour caramel over chocolate chips and let rest for 5 minutes. Whisk until chocolate is melted and ganache has a smooth, glossy finish.

6. Cool at room temperature for 4 to 5 hours. Store in refrigerator if not using right away.

SALTED CARAMEL GANACHE

4 ounces semisweet chocolate chips (about ¾ cups)

¼ cup sugar

1½ teaspoons water

½ teaspoons lemon juice

½ cup heavy cream

1 teaspoon coarse salt

1 tablespoon unsalted butter, cut into pieces

FOR VANILLA SUGAR COOKIES

1 Whisk flour and salt together in a medium-sized bowl and set aside.

2 Cream powdered sugar and butter in the bowl of an electric mixer fitted with a paddle attachment, until fluffy. Add eggs and vanilla extract and mix on medium speed until incorporated, making sure to scrape the bottom and sides of the bowl.

3 Add half of the flour mixture and mix on low speed until combined. Repeat with remaining flour mixture.

4 Roll dough into large ball and flatten into a disk. Wrap in plastic wrap and refrigerate for 30 minutes to 1 hour.

5 Remove dough from refrigerator and let rest at room temperature for 5 minutes.

(RECIPE CONTINUES ON PAGE 220)

VANILLA SUGAR COOKIES

2 cups all-purpose flour

⅛ teaspoon salt

⅔ cup powdered sugar

9 tablespoons unsalted butter, softened

2 eggs

1 teaspoon vanilla extract

OPPOSITE: A bright holiday view toward Spaceship Earth during the 2021 EPCOT International Festival of the Holidays.

SPACESHIP EARTH COOKIES WITH SALTED CARAMEL GANACHE

(CONTINUED)

FOR VANILLA SUGAR COOKIES (CONTINUED)

6 Preheat oven to 350°F. Line 2 baking sheets with parchment paper or silicone baking mats.

7 Roll dough on floured surface into a ⅛-inch-thick rectangle. Cut cookies using a 3-inch Spaceship Earth cookie cutter (or a 3½-inch round, fluted cookie cutter).

8 Place cookies on prepared baking sheet. Chill dough in refrigerator for 15 minutes.

9 Bake for 12 minutes, until edges begin to brown. Cool completely on wire rack before filling and icing.

FOR CHOCOLATE SUGAR COOKIES

1 Whisk flour, cocoa powder, and salt together in a medium-sized bowl and set aside.

2 Cream powdered sugar and butter in the bowl of an electric mixer fitted with a paddle attachment, until fluffy. Add egg and vanilla extract and mix on medium speed until incorporated, making sure to scrape the bottom and sides of the bowl.

3 Add half of flour mixture and mix on low speed until combined. Repeat with remaining flour mixture.

4 Roll dough into large ball and flatten into a disk. Wrap in plastic wrap and refrigerate for 30 minutes to 1 hour.

5 Remove dough from refrigerator and let rest at room temperature for 5 minutes.

6 Preheat oven to 350°F. Line 2 baking sheets with parchment paper or silicone baking mats.

CHOCOLATE SUGAR COOKIES

2 cups all-purpose flour

½ cup unsweetened cocoa powder

½ teaspoon salt

1 cup powdered sugar

¾ cup unsalted butter, softened

1 egg

1 teaspoon vanilla extract

ABOVE and OPPOSITE: Red and sparkly Mickey Mouse ornaments display some holiday cheer, 2010.

7 Roll dough on floured surface into a ⅛-inch-thick rectangle. Cut cookies using a 3-inch Spaceship Earth cookie cutter (or a 3½-inch round, fluted cookie cutter).

8 Place cookies on prepared baking sheet. Chill dough in refrigerator for 15 minutes.

9 Bake for 12 minutes, until edges begin to brown. Cool completely on wire rack before filling and icing.

FOR FILLING COOKIES

Place 1 tablespoon Salted Caramel Ganache on top of each Chocolate Sugar Cookie. Place Vanilla Sugar Cookie on top of ganache and press until ganache spreads to the edge. Refrigerate for 20 to 30 minutes.

FOR ROYAL ICING

Combine powdered sugar, meringue powder, corn syrup, and lemon juice in a large bowl. Stir in water. If icing is still thick, slowly add up to an additional 1 tablespoon water until smooth. Cover with plastic wrap until ready to use.

TO SERVE

Dip Vanilla Sugar Cookie side into Royal Icing. If necessary, wipe excess frosting off edges. Dip in silver sanding sugar. Allow 15 minutes to dry before eating.

ROYAL ICING

3 cups unsifted powdered sugar

1 tablespoon meringue powder

1 tablespoon light corn syrup

1 tablespoon lemon juice

¼ cup water

½ cup silver sanding sugar, for serving

ACKNOWLEDGMENTS

With every single Disney cookbook, I always first thank Karen McClintock, my compatriot in the Disney cookbook world for more than three decades. She is my (not-so) secret ingredient! Gratitude to Katie Wilson for both testing recipes and her amazing organizational skills as we combed through hundreds of recipes from the Walt Disney World Resort and Disneyland Resort festivals to share with you the best of the best. And to our star photography team of Matt Stroshane and James Kilby who have been capturing beautiful food photos for so many festivals. Their creativity and energy is boundless. Jennifer Eastwood, thank you for your brilliance, your patience, and for always listening.

—Pam Brandon

THIS BOOK'S PRODUCERS WOULD LIKE TO SPECIALLY THANK Becky Ballentine, Rebecca Cline, Alyce Diamandis, Katie Farmand, Michele Fortier, Shelby Grasser, Kiran Jeffery, James Kilby, Debra Kohls, Mark LaVine, Ryan March, Karen McClintock, Wendy Meyers, David Nguyen, Chris Ostrander, David Roark, Kevin P. Rafferty, Stacy Salazar, Jeremy Schoolfield, Whitney Simmons, Karlos Siquieros, Matt Stroshane, Lindsay Swantek, Janice Thomson, Steven Vagnini, Michael Vargo, Cayla Ward, Katie Wilson, Jennifer Woods, and Juleen Woods.

ALSO THANK YOU TO THOSE AT DISNEY PUBLISHING: Nancee Adams, Jennifer Black, Christine Choi, Ann Day, Monique Diman-Riley, Jennifer Flagg, Kelly Forsythe, Michael Freeman, Susan Gerber, Alison Giordano, Daneen Goodwin, Tyra Harris, Winnie Ho, Jackson Kaplan, Kim Knueppel, Vicki Korlishin, Kaitie Leary, Meredith Lisbin, Warren Meislin, Scott Piehl, Rachel Rivera, Zan Schneider, Alexandra Serrano, Fanny Sheffield, Dina Sherman, Megan Speer-Levi, Jenny Spring, Pat Van Note, Lynn Waggoner, Jessie Ward, and Rudy Zamora.

INDEX

Index of Recipe Sources

ABOVE: A topiary of Elsa takes a stand at the 2015 EPCOT International Flower & Garden Festival.

BIBLIOGRAPHY & SOURCES

BOOKS

Allan, Graham; and Rebecca Cline and Charlie Price. *Holiday Magic at the Disney Parks: Celebrations Around the World from Fall to Winter*. Los Angeles • New York: Disney Editions, 2020.

Brandon, Pam; and the Disney Chefs, with commemorative contributions by Marcy Carriker Smothers and essays by the Staff of the Walt Disney Archives. *Delicious Disney: Disneyland: Recipes & Stories from The Happiest Place on Earth*. Los Angeles • New York: Disney Editions, 2023.

Brandon, Pam; and Marcy Carriker Smothers and the Disney Chefs. *Delicious Disney: Walt Disney World: Recipes & Stories from The Most Magical Place on Earth*. Los Angeles • New York: Disney Editions, 2021.

Brandon, Pam; and the Disney Chefs. *The Official Disney Parks Cookbook: 101 Magical Recipes from the Delicious Disney Vault*. Los Angeles • New York: Disney Editions, 2022.

_____. *Delicious Disney: The Fresh Edition*. Los Angeles • New York: Disney Editions, 2019.

_____. *Disney Festivals Cookbook: 50 New Recipes, 6 Fabulous Festivals*. Lake Buena Vista, Florida • Anaheim, California: The Walt Disney Company, 2018.

_____. *Disney Food and Wine Festivals Coast to Coast Cookbook—Disney California Adventure & EPCOT*. Lake Buena Vista, Florida • Anaheim, California: The Walt Disney Company, 2017.

_____. *The Best of EPCOT Festivals Cookbook*. Lake Buena Vista, Florida • Anaheim, California: The Walt Disney Company, 2016.

_____. *Delicious Disney: Sweet Treats*. Los Angeles • New York: Disney Editions, 2016.

_____. *EPCOT International Food & Wine Festival [2015]: Recipes & Stories Celebrating 20 Years*. Lake Buena Vista, Florida • Anaheim, California: The Walt Disney Company, 2015.

_____. *A Cooking Safari with Mickey: Recipes from Disney's Animal Kingdom Theme Park and Disney's Animal Kingdom Lodge*. Los Angeles • New York: Disney Editions, 2015.

_____. *A Taste of EPCOT: Festival Food from Around the Globe Cookbook*. Lake Buena Vista, Florida • Anaheim, California: The Walt Disney Company, 2014.

_____. *Kitchen Magic with Mickey: Favorite Recipes from the Disney Parks and Cruise Ships*. Los Angeles • New York: Disney Editions, 2014.

_____. *EPCOT International Food & Wine Festival [2013] Cookbook: Taste Your Way Around the World*. Lake Buena Vista, Florida • Anaheim, California: The Walt Disney Company, 2013.

_____. *EPCOT International Food & Wine Festival [2012] Cookbook: Taste Your Way Around the World*. Lake Buena Vista, Florida • Anaheim, California: The Walt Disney Company, 2012.

_____. *Delicious Disney: Holidays*. New York: Disney Editions, 2012.

_____. *EPCOT International Food & Wine Festival [2011] Cookbook: Passport to a World of Flavors*. Lake Buena Vista, Florida • Anaheim, California: The Walt Disney Company, 2011.

_____. *Delicious Disney: Just for Kids*. New York: Disney Editions, 2011.

_____. *EPCOT International Food & Wine Festival [2010] Cookbook: Celebrating 15 Years of Delicious Discoveries*. Lake Buena Vista, Florida • Anaheim, California: The Walt Disney Company, 2010.

_____. *Chef Mickey: Treasures from the Vault & Delicious New Favorites*. New York: Disney Editions, 2010.

_____. *EPCOT International Food & Wine Festival [2009] Cookbook: 50 Most Requested Recipes of the EPCOT International Food & Wine Festival*. Lake Buena Vista, Florida • Anaheim, California: The Walt Disney Company, 2009.

_____. *EPCOT International Food & Wine Festival [2008] Cookbook: 25 Select Festival Favorite Recipes from Past and Present*. Lake Buena Vista, Florida • Anaheim, California: The Walt Disney Company, 2008.

_____. *Delicious Disney: Desserts*. New York: Disney Editions, 2008.

_____. *Delicious Disney.* New York: Disney Editions, 2006.

_____. *Cooking with Mickey and the Disney Chefs: Recipes from Walt Disney World Resort, Disneyland Resort, and Disney Cruise Line.* New York: Disney Editions, 2004.

_____. *Cooking with Mickey and the Chefs of Walt Disney World Resort.* New York: Hyperion, 1998.

Disney Chefs. *Mickey's Gourmet Cookbook: The Most Popular Recipes from Walt Disney World and Disneyland.* New York: Hyperion, 1994.

_____. *Cooking with Mickey—Gourmet Mickey Cookbook: The Most Requested Recipes from Walt Disney World and Disneyland, Volume II.* Lake Buena Vista, Florida • Anaheim, California: The Walt Disney Company, 1991.

_____. *Cooking with Mickey Around Our World: The MOST Requested Recipes from Walt Disney World and Disneyland.* Lake Buena Vista, Florida • Anaheim, California: The Walt Disney Company, 1986.

Smith, Dave; and Steven Vagnini. *Disney A to Z: The Official Encyclopedia, Sixth Edition.* Los Angeles • New York: Disney Editions, 2023.

IMAGE CREDITS

All images in this book courtesy **Yellow Shoes Marketing Resource Center.**

ABOVE: Walt Disney World Resort chefs prepare trays of cinnamon buns for the France pavilion in World Showcase at EPCOT, 2015.

MORE RECIPES FROM THE
DELICIOUS
DISNEY
VAULT

For more information, visit Books.Disney.com/series/Delicious-Disney

DISNEY EDITIONS